施璐德亚洲有限公司 编

施璐德年鉴 2016

VISION DRIVEN LIFE

CNOOD 2008 TO 2016

复旦大学出版社

CNOOD Yearbook (2016)

1
记 2017 年施璐德年会
The 2017 Annual Meeting of CNOOD
Loreen

15
从心出发
Start from the Heart
Dennis

22
致诚，致爱，致心——成长于 CNOOD
The Commitment of Sincerity, Love and Heart—Growing at CNOOD
Fay

30
施璐德年鉴（2016）
CNOOD Yearbook（2016）
Andy

34
存至信，一片祥云
Cherish the Utmost Trust, and There Will Come a Propitious Cloud
Chemmary

38
来过 CNOOD
I Have Been in CNOOD
Connor

43
我眼中的施璐德
What I know about CNOOD
Cristhian Allende

46
启　程
Starting on a New Journey
Dannie

49
2016 年年鉴
Eric

51
施璐德亚洲有限公司董事长候选人申请
Applying for Candidacy for Chairman of Board of CNOOD ASIA LIMITED
Dennis

57
CEO 就职演讲
CEO Inaugural Speech
Fay

64
CNOOD 首任 CEO 就职典礼圆满举行
Inaugural Ceremony of CNOOD's First CEO Held with Great Success
Loreen

78
行 走
Walking
Jeff Xu

80
新芽在这里成长，梦想从这里起航
Here is the Place Where New Buds Grow, and Dreams Start
Jenna

84
质量卓越 | 价格最优 | 服务真诚 | 持续改进
Supreme Quality | Superior Price | Sincere Service | Sustaining Improvement
Lay

89
一个无边际的系统
A System without Boundary
Nick

93
从开端到另一个开端
From One Beginning to Another
Billy

97
在施璐德工作的体会
WORKING AT CNOOD
Nicolas Kipreos

101
CNOOD 的魅力
The Charm of CNOOD
Tiger

105
2016-CNOOD 印象
2016-CNOOD IMPRESSIONS
Tony

115
人生如戏，CNOOD 是我的舞台
Life Is Like a Drama,
and CNOOD Is My Stage
Sissi

121
峥嵘岁月
Uncommon Days
Lee Thompson

124
小白的梦想
The Dreams of a Rookie
Beny Wang

129
A Partir del Corazón,
Comienza el mundo
Dennis

134
自由而无用的灵魂——CNOOD 自序
Free and Useless Souls—Preface to
CNOOD Yearbook
Dennis

147
2016 心路历程之感言
Thoughts on the Journey of Heart in 2016
Ben Tam

156
CNOOD DOCS DEPT.2016 感想
Impressions of CNOOD Documents
Department in 2016
Angela, Cindy & Tina

158
光阴悠悠自难忘
Long, Unforgettable Times
Echo Lee

161
桥流水不流
It is the Bridge that Flows,
Not the Water
Echo Lee

167
一次日出
A Sunrise
Lilia Chen

169

CNOOD——还原倒立的世界
CNOOD: Restoring the Upside-down World
Tina Zhang

175

塞尔维亚——造梦开始的地方
Serbia, Where We Begin to Create Dreams
Tina Zhang

183

患难之交见真情
成功就是跌倒九次、站起十回
A friend in need is a friend indeed!
Success is falling nine times and getting up ten
Wael Ismail

185

亚沙·感悟——一路有你
You Are Always with Us: Reflection on the "Asian-Pacific Business Schools Desert Challenge"
Dennis

198

特别的爱给父亲
Special Love to My Father
Tong Ming

201

施璐德集团公司年鉴
CNOOD 2017 To 2016
施璐德财务部
CNOOD Accounting Department

记 2017 年施璐德年会
The 2017 Annual Meeting of CNOOD

■ Loreen

新春年会：从心出发，成就梦想

2017年1月12日，施璐德 2017 年新春年会在上海兴国宾馆 8 号会议中心拉开了帷幕。与往年一样，此次新春年会一般包括 3 个部分，时间一共持续在 7 天左右，即展示与交流、歌舞联欢与游览、实践学习与展望。每一年的年会对施璐德来说都至关重要，因为它不仅是一次总领性

New Year Annual Meeting: Starting from the Heart, Fulfilling the Dreams

On January 12, 2017, the New Year Annual Meeting of CNOOD opened in Villa Eight Conference Center, Radisson Blu Plaza Xing Guo Hotel Shanghai. As usual, the meeting would last about seven days and include three parts: presentation and communication; song-and-dance party

的会议，它更是一个团圆的节日，世界各地的施璐德人都会在此汇聚。同时，还会邀请一些关心我们的朋友、和我们一起奋进的合作伙伴、平日里默默付出最支持我们的家属一起来联欢与见证。

大家庭世界各地齐相聚

年会第一部分，展示与交流。

首先由 Fay Lee 致欢迎词，欢迎和感谢西班牙分公司 CNOOD ENGINEERING S.L.、南美分公司 CNOOD LATAM SPA、香港分公司 CNOOD HONG KONG LIMITED、常熟分工厂 CNOOD EQUIPMENT MANUFACTURING CO., LTD 的各位同事以及从世界各地辛苦奔波、远道而来的国内外合伙人。随后各分公司给大家简要介绍了其近况与各公司的特色、专长等，分享了过去一年的经验与成果。通过这样的展示与交流，促进了施璐德内部各分公司之间的了解，加深了同事之间的感情，增强了施璐德这个大家庭的凝集力。

and sight-seeing; practical learning and prospect. Every year's annual meeting is of great importance to CNOOD, not only as a meeting that sets the pace for the company, but also as carnival for reunion when all its members from all over the world get together. Meanwhile, we invite friends who care for us, cooperative partners who advance alongside us and family members who support us with silent sacrifice on a daily basis to have fun together and witness our achievements.

Members of a Big Family Came together from the World

The first part of the annual meeting: presentation and communication.

At the beginning, Fay Lee gave a welcome speech, expressing our gratitude to colleagues from branch companies: CNOOD ENGINEERING S.L. from Spain, CNOOD LATAM SPA from South America, CNOOD HONG KONG LIMITED, and CNOOD EQUIPMENT MANUFACTURING CO., LTD from Changshu, as well as our partners who had traveled a long way from various countries. After the speech, all the branch companies briefly introduced their recent developments with their distinguishing features and expertise, and shared with everyone their experience and achievements in the past year. Through the presentation and communication, the branch companies within CNOOD knew each other better; the friendship between colleagues was strengthened; and the cohesion of the big family of CNOOD was reinforced.

国内外共进伙伴展风采

在各分公司交流结束后，我们邀请了部分在过去一年给予我们莫大支持与帮助的合作伙伴和朋友进行了展示，共谋未来。小编就不在这里一一列举了，但是这份恩情，都将铭记在每一个施璐德人的心里。

Cooperative Partners from Home and Abroad Displayed Their Glamour

After the branch companies finished their sharing, we invited some of our cooperative partners and friends, who had offered us huge support and help during the past tear, to give presentation on future cooperation. I cannot list all the names here, but every CNOOD member will bear in mind our gratitude toward them.

西子湖畔把酒言欢　歌舞小品其乐融融

　　结束了两天紧凑而丰富的展示与交流，紧接着我们大批人马乘大巴从上海出发前往美丽的西子湖畔。白天赏湖光山色，晚上就进入了年会最热闹的部分啦——歌舞联欢晚会。2017年联欢晚会的主题是"时光旧影，重回1920"，1920是民国风哦，嘿嘿！小编知道，在此再多的言语都不及一大波美图来得深刻，准备接图。

Beside the West Lake We Enjoyed Wine and Chat; With Sing and Dancing, Our Happiness Knew No Bounds

　　We left Shanghai and headed for the beautiful West Lake as soon as the two-day colorful, well-organized presentation and communication concluded. We enjoyed the scenery of the lake and hills during the day; when night fell, we entered the liveliest part of the meeting: sing-and-dance party. The theme of this year's party was "Impressions of Old Day—Back to 1920". By the way, the year 1920 meant a retro style. I understand that at this moment any words would invariably pale beside a good number of nice pictures. So, get ready!

小编点评：新人的开场舞热情洋溢；萱萱的舞蹈每年都有惊喜；Dennis 每年年会必拉的小提琴，今年终于成功发出悦耳的琴声，夺得掌声一片；乌克兰同（美）事（女）吟诗一首，没太听懂，可是有颜就好。

Editor's Comment: The opening dance by new members were brimming with enthusiasm; Xuanxuan's dancing surprised us every year; Dennis' violin, which he played on every and each annual meeting, finally succeeded in producing pleasant sounds this year, wining a big applause; Our Ukrainian colleague, a pretty lady, recited a poem that I did not quite follow, but her superb appearance alone was sufficient.

小编点评：LU 献唱西语歌曲，引 "狼"（热情洋溢的西语系合伙人）共舞；CNOOD 小萌宝们，一曲《大王叫我来巡山》调皮可爱；纳尼？他们竟然在朗诵《再别康桥》！！

Editor's Comment: LU sang a Spanish song while dancing with "wolves" (enthusiastic Spanish-speaking partners); Cute CNOOD kids sang together *The King Asked Me to Patrol the Mountain*; What? They were reciting *Saying Goodbye to Cambridge Again*!

小编点评：街舞达人 Thompson 的 Popping 灵活动感，谁说工科男只会搬砖；才女 Helena 去年吉他今年筝；两位绅士 Paul 和 Billy 温柔对唱世纪经典；Martin 情歌动人，酒不醉人人自醉！

Editor's Comment: The agile and dynamic popping performance of Thompson, a master of street dance, convinced us that engineering guy is capable not only of writing dull codes; Helena, a talented girl who performed guitar last year, played Chinese zither for us this year; Two gentlemen, Paul and Billy, sang to each other a classic song of the century; Martin's love song deeply moved all the people, who were drunk not by wine but by themselves.

大奖不断送最美新春祝福

今年的抽奖环节在常规的一、二、三等奖和特等奖的基础上，增设了一个温暖的环节——"Love·Culture Transmission"。即每个人都可以根据自愿原则，准备一份礼物承载着你的记忆、理念以及你赋予的期许或其他特殊含义，随机抽取送给那个有缘人。

Many a Prize Sent the Best Wishes for New Year

In the lucky draw section of this year, in addition to the routine First, Second, Third Prizes and the Special Prize, there was a newly added heartwarming feature—"Love·Culture Transmission", where you could voluntarily prepare a gift that carried your memory, idea, expectation or other special meanings on it. The gift was then randomly selected and given to the one who was tied up with you by destiny.

小编点评：这个意味着年会中奖概率至少超过50%了，然而小编这么多年，依然没有中奖，苍天呐！

Editor's Comment: So, it meant that we had a chance at least bigger than 50 percent of winning a prize, didn't it? However, I never made it in all these years. Alas!

各大表彰花落最"勤"施璐德人

言归正传,施璐德今天取得的小小成绩,离不开每一位辛勤付出的施璐德人。

Awards to the Most Diligent CNOOD Members

Frankly speaking, the small achievements made by CNOOD today depend heavily upon the diligence and devotion of all its members.

小编点评：Amir 春风化雨，爱人者，人恒爱之；Fay 上善若水，柔德克刚；Tiger 桃李不言，下自成蹊；Jeff 最佳新人，生机无限；Lilia 小虎探道，何惧？

Editor's Comment: Amir was awarded for his salutary influence of education (as the saying goes, one who loves others is always beloved by others); Fay, for her noble character resembling that of water, soft and yet able to subdue the hard; Tiger, for his true worth that attracts admiration; Jeff, as the Best New Employee of the Year, for his boundless vitality; Lilia, for her fearless exploration as a youthful, vigorous member of CNOOD.

小编点评：优秀员工，Angela、Lay、石头、思思众望所归。对了，石头还得了"先锋奖"；Nick、Kent双剑合璧，独领DT（"程序猿"）风骚；项目攻坚，钢结构团队斩获"最佳项目团队"。

Editor's Comment: Angela, Lay, Stone and Sisi were given the Best Employees of the Year Awards, while Stone was also given the Pioneer Award; Nick and Kent made a perfect combination with exceptional performance in data technology; Steel structure team won the Best Team of the Year Award for their outstanding effort in carrying out projects.

小编点评："Work Bench"是什么东东？它是一个拟生态系统，也是一位集大成的"专家"和"老师"，有点类似围棋界的AlphaGo，当然任重道远。具体详情，请咨询CNOOD任何人哦！具体获奖人员，小编就不在这一一点名了，看图！

Editor's Comment: What is Workbench? It is a quasi-ecological system as well as an all-embracing "expert" and "tutor", somewhat similar to AlphaGo in the field of *go*. Of course, there is still heavy tasks and a long way that waits it. For detailed information please refer to anyone in CNOOD. I'm not going to list all the names. Look at the photos!

升职仪式

恭喜 Wales、Shelley、Charles、Ada、Cindy 成功升职！熬过三厘米，功夫不负有心人！

Promotion Ceremony

Congratulations to Wales, Shelley, Charles, Ada and Cindy for their promotion! Hard work pays off when you have successfully endured the difficult times in the first couple of years.

Dennis 致辞

Dennis 说:"给施璐德十年,还一个全新的自己!"如临深渊,如履薄冰,畏惧而勇敢,施璐德一直在创业的路上!

Dennis' Speech

Dennis said, "Give CNOOD ten years, and you'll be an entirely renewed person." Cautious as though walking on the brink of an abyss and treading on thin ice, fearful and yet courageous, CNOOD is always on the way of entrepreneurship!

小编点评:西湖的水,Dennis 的泪!堂堂八尺大汉,他哭了,别问我他为什么眼里饱含泪水,因为他爱得深沉!

Editor's Comment: Shall I compare the tears of Dennis to the water of the West Lake? As a tall, dignified man, he wept. Don't ask me why his eyes were brimming with tears; that's because he loved so deeply!

拍全家福啦!

欢乐的时光总是过得很快,让我们一起带着感动与感恩大步迈向崭新的2017年吧!

Time for a Photo of the Whole Family

Happy time was always short. With a moved heart and gratitude, let's stride toward the brand-new year of 2017!

小编点评：与君共饮，拉手拍照，一百年不许变！

Editor's Comment: We drank wine together, and took photos hand in hand. May the friendship last for a hundred years!

罗蓉
Loreen

Loreen，2014年硕士毕业于东华大学，随后正式加入施璐德。性格活泼开朗，但也冷静沉着。最害怕被"大众"同化，希望永葆独立的精神和不怕做奇葩的事情。

Loreen formally joined CNOOD soon after graduating from Donghua University with a master's degree in 2014. With a lively and cheerful disposition, she is also calm and cool-headed. What she fears most is being assimilated by "the masses". She hopes to maintain the spirit of independence forever, never afraid of doing "weird" things.

从心出发
Start from the Heart

■ Dennis

从 2009 年 9 月 18 日算起，CNOOD 公司已经七载有余。期间，志同道合者、勇猛精进者、孜孜以求者不断增加；当然，志得意满者、疏于进取者、各种矛盾也不断增加。CNOOD 的现状怎样？目标为何？发展思路是什么？如何展开？

八年以前，CNOOD 呱呱坠地，五个人，有费凤，有费凤她妈妈，有费凤她儿子，有文涛，还有我；佟哥在看着我们，Shirley 在盯着我们。我们每个人带着四颗心：爱心、上进心、自信心和平常心。

2009 年 7 月，CNOOD 签署第一个合同，客户是 SALZIGITTA。10 月，与

As of September 18, 2009, CNOOD has now well passed the seventh year. During this course, we have more and more companions who share the same vision, who are courageous and enterprising, and who pursue their dreams with perseverance. Nevertheless, we have at the same time met more and more persons who are complacent with their achievement, and who are no longer eager to make progress. Various conflicts have also increased. What is the current situation of CNOOD? What is its goal? What is its strategy of development? How will the strategy be carried out?

Eight years ago when CNOOD was born, we had in total five persons: Fei Feng, Fei Feng's mother, Fei Feng's son, Wen Tao and me. Kevin Tong was looking at us, and Shirley was staring at us. Everyone of us had four words engraved in the heart: love, ambition, confidence, and tranquility.

In July 2009, CNOOD signed its first ever contract, the client being SALZIGITTA.

TOTAL NIGERIA 签署第一个合同。11月，与 THYSSENCRRUB VIETNAM 签署第一个合同。

2010 年 8 月，Jet 加入。3 月，与 CUNADO 签署第一个合同。4 月，与 GEONET GROUP 签署第一个合同。7 月，与 ARCELORMITTAL 签署第一个合同。年底，Shirley 因家庭事业发展原因，正式离开 CNOOD。

2011 年 2 月，Auhuan 加入。3 月，Tiger 加入。8 月 Tina Jiang 加入。10 月 Wendy 加入。5 月与 JUAN GABRIEL 开始一系列合作。8 月，CNOOD 在 Kevin 的坚持下，赢得第一个万吨项目。10 月第一个万吨项目成功完成。

2012 年 1 月，Fay 加入。至此，CNOOD 公司架构功能板块基本形成。5 月，与 GSL 合作。5 月，Amir 加入。6 月，终止与 Jet 的合作。10 月，Joy 加入。

2013 年 4 月，为期一年的 PDVSA 项目成功完成。10 月，终止与 Joy 的合作。

2014 年 1 月，Mario、Nico、Cristian 和 Gino 加入，CNOOD LATAM SPA 成立。2 月，与 IMI 签署第一个合同。3 月，Tina Xu 加入。5 月，IMI 第一个合同成功完成。5 月，常熟工厂开工。6 月，与 SKYWARD 签署第一个合同。7 月，Wael 加入。8 月与 HUTA MARINE 签署第一个合同。8 月，Neo 加入。9 月，

In October, it signed the first contract with TOTAL NIGERIA and in November with THYSSENCRRUB VIETNAM.

In August 2010, Jet joined us. In March, CNOOD signed the first contract with CUANDO; in April, it signed the first contract with GEONET GROUP and in July with ARCELORMITTAL. At the end of the year, Shirley officially resigned from CNOOD for family and career considerations.

In February 2011, Auhuan joined us. In March, Tiger joined us, and in August Tina Jiang, in October Wendy. In May, CNOOD initiated a series of cooperation with JUAN GABRIEL. In August, thanks to Kevin's persistence, CNOOD won a ten-thousand-ton project, which was concluded with success in October.

In January 2012, Fay joined us. Thus the functional structure of the company was basically established. In May, CNOOD began the cooperation with GSL. Amir joined us in the same month. In June, CNOOD terminated the cooperation with Jet. In October, Joy joined us.

In April 2013, the one-year-long project with PDVSA was concluded with success. In October, CNOOD terminated the cooperation with Joy.

In January 2014, Mario, Nico, Cristian and Gino joined us. CNOOD LATAM SPA was set up in the same month. In February, CNOOD signed the first contract with IMI. In March, Tina Xu joined us. In May, the first contract with IMI was carried out with success. In the same month, Changshu Processing Center began its operation. In

与SUEZ CANAL签署第一个合同。10月，Pat加入。12月，CNOOD HK LTD成立。

2015年1月，与BELFI签署第一个合同。3月，与YPFB签署第一个合同。6月，Chin加入。7月Esteban加入。9月，CNOOD ENGINEERING SPA成立。

2016年1月，签署第一个钢结构合同。6月，Ben加入。8月，Christian Allende加入。10月PAUL加入。12月，Tina Zhang加入。自此，CNOOD全球的市场布局初步形成。市场涉及领域：石油、天然气、矿山、水处理、新能源和基础设施。

步步走来，如履薄冰。如何心思，作何决定，步步惊心。没有前车之鉴，全赖跟随内心。勤锻炼，多思索，爱学习。不故步自封，不因噎废食。人品问题，当断则断；错误频仍，有则改之。在探索中学习，在追求中进步。

事业提升，至善至真。唯至善，方久

June, CNOOD signed the first contract with SKYWARD. In July, Wael joined us. In August, CNOOD signed the first contract with HUTA MARINE. Neo joined us in the same month. In September, CNOOD signed the first contract with SUEZ CANAL. In October, Pat joined us. In December, CNOOD HK LTD was set up.

In January 2015, CNOOD signed the first contract with BELFI and in March the first contract with YPFB. In June, Chin joined us and in July Esteban. In September, CNOOD ENGINEERING SPA was set up.

In January 2016, CNOOD signed its first contract of steel structure product. In June, Ben joined us. In August, Christian Allende joined us. In October, Paul joined us. In December, Tina Zhang joined us. Thus CNOOD had preliminarily established a business layout across global markets, covering areas including oil, gas, mines, water, new energies and infrastructure.

Step by step, we have come a long way with great precaution, as if treading on the thin ice. We constantly feel startled in our thinking and decision-making. Lacking the experience of predecessors from which we can learn, we depend entirely on following the inner voice of heart. Practice more, think more, and learn more. Do not rest on your laurels. Never give up for fear of a small obstacle. Do not hesitate to cut off the relations with persons who have moral problems. While there are frequent errors, correct them every time you find one. Let's learn in our exploration, and advance in our pursuit.

The promotion of business depends on

长；唯至真，感人深。至善事业方能久长，至真待人方能感人。至善无大小，莫以善小而不为；至真无巨细，莫以恶小而为之。积少成多，积土成山，积善成德。《周易》言之："天行健，君子以强不息；地势坤，君子以厚德载物。"

至善事业，无有背景？全靠人品。仁义礼智信，众所周知，众所景仰。切实兴之，合作者至，支持者众，事兴业起。成王败寇，实一时之风气；始皇长城，非万古之基业。夫子仁义，德沛千古；孟子道德，延以千年。非强制，非苟且，非盲从，非欺瞒。大浪淘沙，沉者为金；千古传承，至善至真。循循善诱，行无声之教；惇惇教诲，聚众人之势。以至善聚人，得以乘势；以至真待人，得以延势。乘势，事得以成；延势，事得以广。

the supreme good and the supreme sincerity. Only with the supreme good can our cause last long; and only with the supreme sincerity can we move others. To achieve the supreme good, big or small, never fail to do good thing even it is trivial. To achieve the supreme sincerity, big or small, never engage in evil even it is trivial. As the saying goes, "Many a little makes a mickle." We can make a mountain by piling up earth, and fulfill virtue by accumulating good deeds. It is said in *Book of Changes*: "In accordance with the vigorous motion of heaven, the superior man ceaselessly strive to become stronger; in accordance with the power of the earth, the superior man with his great virtue takes on greater responsibilities."

What if we don't have favorable background in the cause of the supreme good? Depend solely on moral quality: benevolence, righteousness, courtesy, wisdom and honesty, which are well known and admired by all. If we effectively put them into practice, companions will automatically come to work with us, and we will win many supporters, helping our business to prosper. "The winner takes it all" is but a temporary phenomenon, and the Great Wall built by Qin Shihuang (the first emperor of the Qin Dynasty) is by no means an eternal achievement. The virtue and morality advocated by Confucius and Mencius have been handed down for thousands of years and have benefited all people throughout the history. This is not about compulsion, drifting along, blind obedience or cheating. When big waves wash sands, it is the gold that is deposited.

　　事在人为，意者，事业兴盛败亡之核心；人者，事业兴盛败亡之关键。意者，爱也。爱心育人，爱心待人，爱心做事。爱人，则责己以周，虑人以全。责己以周，事无巨细，面面俱到，成事可期。虑人以全，事无巨细，面面俱到，佳业可成。人者，团队也。团队培育，从幼年始，以壮为伍，俟老年终，有始有终。以幼为师，清明澄澈，心思纯净，不杂污染；以壮为伍，兢兢业业，孜孜以求，生机勃勃；以老为师，心思缜密，经验老到，虑无不及。团队多寡，并非关键，意字当先，爱字当先，跟随内心，做则能优，做则能强。无意则无神，泯然如众人。是以，以小团队，泛爱众心，组织架构，因地制宜，因时制宜，则做无不成。

Throughout the history, only the supreme good and the supreme sincerity have been passed down from generation to generation. They influence people with patient guidance, like the rain silently penetrating the earth; their earnest and tireless teachings gather the power of people. If you gain the support of people by the supreme good, you can take advantage of opportunities and therefore achieve your goals; if you treat people with the supreme sincerity, you can extend the possibility and then expand your business.

　　All things depend on the effort of people. People are the key to the success or failure of our business, while their willingness is at the core of all factors that determine the rise and fall of a cause. By willingness we mean love, with which we nurture people, treat people and do business. To love people is to be strict with ourselves and considerate to others in every aspect, big or small. Then we can expect the achievement of our goal and the success of our business. By people we mean team. The creation of a team is a task that we shall carry through to the end, during which we learn from people of different ages: we learn from children whose mind are crystal-clear and innocent without pollution; we work with adult companions who are assiduous and energetic in their never-ending pursuit; we learn from the old who consider in a thorough manner with their prudent thoughts and rich experience. It is not important whether we have many or few members in our team. It is the willingness of people and love that we should put first. Following the heart we can excel and become strong. Without willingness we will lose our

创业成功之路，合众力，聚众心，努力坚持，处之泰然，假以时日，功遂名成。不以物喜，不以己悲，以恒常心为创业心，时时在创业，事事在创业，则步步进，日日升。倘若瞻前顾后，首鼠两端，事事为失败作打算，时时为后路作准备，人之生日有限，如何有时为成事作谋划。

施璐德，实锻炼之基石，创业之平台，伙伴之基础。用心做，百炼成钢；用心处，千世伙伴；用心行，万世基业。举众之力，以己先行；举众之行，率先垂范。想人所想，急人所急，处人所处。己所不欲，勿施于人。责己以周，虑人以宽。如是，则事业可期。

给施璐德10年，换一个全新的自己，处一个百炼成钢的团队。

从心出发，一直在创业的路上。

spirit, and wind up as a mediocre company. Therefore, we will succeed in whatever we do if we create a team of small size but with fraternity and structure it in a flexible way to adapt to different circumstances.

If we are able to collect the power and mind of people, and remain calm in our persistent effort on the way of entrepreneurship, success is only a matter of time. Do not be pleased by external gains or saddened by personal losses. Maintain a normal mentality and engage in entrepreneurship at every time in everything, making progress every day with every step. But if we are overcautious and indecisive, always preparing for possible failures in the future, how can we find time to plan for achieving things in a limited life?

CNOOD is indeed a firm foundation for practice, a platform for entrepreneurship, and a base for partnership. Always do things with all our heart, then we can become as strong as steel, encounter companions for a lifetime, and lay the solid foundation for future development. If we want to gain the support of others, we should first set an example by ourselves. Think for others as if it were our own matter; search for solution for others as if it were our own problem; and put ourselves in the situation as others do. As the saying goes, "Don't do unto others what you would not want done unto you." Be strict with ourselves and lenient toward others. By so doing, we can expect to fulfill our goals.

Please give CNOOD ten years, in exchange of a totally different future for you, and an invincible team.

Starting from the heart, we are forever on the way of entrepreneurship.

池勇海，男，汉族，1970年出生于湖北仙桃。先后毕业于武汉理工大学、复旦大学，获管理学硕士学位、经济学博士学位。

他是一名跨国公司的创立人、执行董事。他致力于构筑一个平台，打造一个共创、共享、共治的无边界的有机生态系统。让每一位在这个平台上的国内外合伙人、员工都能在这里成长、壮大成为未来的CEO。

他也是一个"屌丝"，上演了一场真正的屌丝逆袭。从农村里走出来的孩子，羞涩，不自信，哑巴英语到国际谈判中的从容、睿智、优雅的转身。

他是一个造梦者，他告诉身边的每一个人，无论你是想做一个业界精英、老板CEO或是哲学家、诗人、乞丐都可以。心有多远，你就能走多远！

他更是一个履梦人，为了实现自己的"中国梦"，先后造访了乌克兰、德国、伊朗、叙利亚、印度尼西亚、智利、澳大利亚、伊拉克、美国、土耳其、厄瓜多尔、尼日利亚、印度、埃及、沙特、巴拿马、玻利维亚等数十个国家。他用他的双脚丈量着世界，也用他的梦想为中国制造与中国创造走向世界贡献自己的力量。

Born in Xiantao, Hubei Province in 1970, Dennis Chi is of Han nationality and graduated from Wuhan University of Technology with a master's degree in Management Science and from Fudan University with a doctoral degree in Economics.

He is the founder and executive director of a multinational company, devoting himself to building a platform and an organic ecosystem without boundary, which is created, shared and managed by all its members, so that every partner, domestic or foreign, as well as every employee, can grow stronger to become a future CEO.

He used to be a "loser"; however, he performed a real counterattack. Once a shy, unconfident boy from the countryside with extremely poor English speaking proficiency, he has transformed into a business leader who shows calmness, wisdom and grace in international negotiations.

He is a dream-maker who tells everyone around him: "You could be any kind of person, be it professional elite, boss, CEO, or be it philosopher, poet, and beggar— whatever. You can go as far as your heart goes!"

He is also a dream-fulfiller who, in order to realize his "Chinese Dream", has visited dozens of countries: Ukraine, Germany, Iran, Syria, Indonesia, Chile, Australia, Iraq, USA, Turkey, Ecuador, Nigeria, India, Egypt, Saudi Arabia, Panama, Bolivia, etc. He measures the world with his feet, and with his dreams he makes contribution to pushing Chinese manufacture and Chinese creation to the world.

池勇海
Dennis

致诚，致爱，致心——成长于 CNOOD
The Commitment of Sincerity, Love and Heart—Growing at CNOOD

■ Fay

历经八个春秋，在持续发展和转型中的 CNOOD 是一个怎么样的状态呢？每个人都会有自己的理解、体悟。认识 CNOOD 七年，身在 CNOOD 五年余，我不断更新对她的认知，参与她的发展，而她亦陪伴我成长。

她，兼收并蓄，生机勃勃。唯快不破，唯勤不破，唯信不破。

她，是一个互相关心、创造开心的大家庭。

她，是一个共创、共享、共治的无边界的有机生态系统。

在这里，我们希望：

（1）每一位 CNOOD 人都是平等的，犹如一颗颗种子，可以主动利用一切资源向着个人成长目标快速发展；

（2）每一位 CNOOD 人有着各自的优势特点，大家可以寻找属于自己的成长轨

What is CNOOD like in constant development and transformation during the eight years? Everyone has his/her own understanding. I have known CNOOD for seven years, and have been with her for more than five years. I have been continuously renewing my knowledge of her and participating in her development, while she has also been accompanying me in my growth.

It is all-embracing and full of vitality. Only speed, diligence and integrity cannot be defeated.

CNOOD is a big family whose members care for each other and create delightfulness.

CNOOD is an organic ecosystem without boundary, which is created, shared and managed by all her members.

Here, we hope that:

(1) All the CNOOD members are equal, like seeds, rapidly developing towards their personal goals of growth by actively using all the resources available.

(2) All the CNOOD members have their

迹。先成长起来的人可以给后来者传授经验和技术，不同领域的可以发挥各自专业优势相互支持与分享，从而实现全员的共同成长与发展；

（3）每一位 CNOOD 人都能站在创业者的角度去思考问题，解决问题，将自己视为公司的主人之一，都能得到公司其他人的全力支持。每一位 CNOOD 人都是这个生态系统的最大受益人，其成长和发展都依赖于这个系统。

（4）每一位 CNOOD 人需秉承致诚、致爱、致心的胸襟。我们将以诚自律、以爱互信、以心明理，不断地完善自我，不断地革新我们的生态系统。我们需要每个人的努力，需要集体的智慧，让 CNOOD 更加优秀更加强大。

own advantages, able to find their own track of growth. Those who grow faster pass on experience and technology to the late-comers, and people in different fields support and share with each other by giving full play to their professional strengths, thus achieving the growth and development of all the members.

(3) All the CNOOD members, seeing themselves as masters of the company, are able to consider and solve problems from the entrepreneurial point of view, and be fully supported by all other members in the company. All the CNOOD members are the biggest beneficiaries of this ecosystem, upon which their growth and development depend.

(4) All the CNOOD members are required the commitment of sincerity, love and heart. We will discipline ourselves with honesty, trust each other with love, and seek the truth by heart. We will continuously perfect ourselves and renovate our ecosystem. We need everyone's effort as well as collective

在我眼里，CNOOD 是一个独特的存在，我期待着她发展、壮大，期待着她成为更多人获得成长、发展、收获辉煌的平台。作为这个系统中的一分子，一直以来，我不断探索，努力守护，希望尽自己的绵薄之力促进 CNOOD 的发展壮大。在这份探索与守护中，在与创始人 Dennis 的明辨中，我逐渐理解并且实践一个个"关键词"的深意，而这些"关键词"也陪伴并见证了我的成长……

关键词："人"

CNOOD 的财富是人，尽全力去满足每个人的成长愿望与需求！

育人即是生财，人才是我们的未来！

因此，公司设立了培训机制与教育基金，分配机制也是"藏富于民"，全员持股，协作机制都围绕这样的目标建立并且实施。

我们在项目中，认识人，发现人才，给予人才更多的资源，帮助他们更好地提升自我，也实现业务能力的不断升级。

（Tips：得失不在一时之间，任何时候做好自己，天道酬勤！）

在一次次与新加入的合伙人的交流

wisdom to make CNOOD a better and stronger company.

In my eyes, CNOOD is a unique being. I wish her to grow stronger, and to be a platform for even more people to grow, develop and achieve glorious performance. As a member of this organization, I have always been exploring and protecting, in the hope that I could do my best to make CNOOD grow stronger. In the meantime, during the inspiring debates with Dennis, the founder of CNOOD, I gradually come to understand the deep meaning of all the "keywords" and put them into practice, which have in turn accompanied and witnessed my growth ...

Keyword: People

The wealth of CNOOD is people. We will do our best to fulfill everyone's wish and needs of growth.

To nurture people is to create wealth. Talents are our future!

Therefore, CNOOD sets up training program and education fund, with an income distribution system designed to "leave the wealth to people". Employee stock ownership plan and coordination mechanism have also been established and carried out to fulfill this objective.

We know people and discover talents in projects; we give them more resources to help them to improve themselves more effectively and to upgrade their business capabilities.

(Tips: Gains and losses do not depend on any short moment. Always be your best self. God will reward the diligent people.)

It becomes clearer to me every time I

中，越来越发现，其实志同道合的人无需太多的修饰，坦诚沟通，你我必然会是一家人。

communicate with newly joined partners that people with a common vision don't need much make-up. We will naturally become a family if we communicate with each other frankly and open-heartedly.

关键词："读书"

《西点军校的领导魂》
《沉思录》
《失控》
《知行合一》
《哲学的盛宴》
《道德经》
《孔子》
《自我实现的宇宙》

我们的书单在增加中，读书，不可辜负！

在CNOOD的办公室里，书籍，是最美丽的风景；读书，是最优雅的行为。

Keyword: Reading

The West Point Way of Leadership
The Meditation of Marcus Aurelius
Out of Control
The Unity of Knowledge and Practice
History of Philosophy
Tao Te Ching
Confucius
Self-Actualizing Cosmos

Our book-list is ever enlarging. Reading should not be betrayed.

In the offices of CNOOD, books are the most beautiful scene, and reading is the most graceful action.

关键词："倾听"

倾听中有专业的知识！
倾听中有实际的问题！
倾听中有真实的需求！
倾听中有全方位的解决方案！

虔诚地去倾听，我们总有机会可以学习更多，理解更多，获得更多的支持，制作更准确的解决方案。

Keyword: Listening

There is professional expertise in listening!
There are practical problems in listening!
There are real demands in listening!
There are comprehensive solutions in listening!

When we devote ourselves to listening, there are always opportunities that we can learn more, understand more, acquire more support, and develop more accurate solutions.

关键词："无用"

放下当下，认真参与一些看似"无用"的会议和拜访，为未来的成长做一些储备。

用心去支持、参与、帮助其他的"无

Keyword: Useless

Forget the current moment. Seriously take part in some "useless" meetings and visits, preparing for future growth.

Support, participate in and help with

关"的项目，积累无处不在。

无心插柳柳成荫，也许这些"无心""无用""无关"，将为我们的未来铺出一条大道。

关键词："放弃"

学会专注，学会坚持，懂得放弃！

我们曾经放弃过的客户，因为他只适合做朋友，不适合合作。

我们曾经放弃过的产品，因为它只会消耗我们的时间。

有时，我们不得不放弃一些伙伴，因为他们的志趣不在此，他们属于另一片天地。

关键词："信任"

信任，这种力量是可以传递的。

当你100%地信任一个人时，他是不想辜负你的。

信任，这种深扎在人们心底的原始情绪是可以相互感染的。

即便是被辜负了，我们也要去感染更多的人。

珍惜每一次的信任，为CNOOD代言，为自己创立口碑。

关键词："模式"

一个可复制的多赢系统！

"irrelevant" projects with all your heart. There is accumulation everywhere.

As the saying goes, "Though you plant a willow unintentionally, it will eventually make a pleasant shade." Perhaps the things we consider as "useless", "irrelevant" or "unintentional" will pave the way for our future.

Keyword: Give up

Learn to concentrate. Learn to persevere. Know when to give up.

We once gave up a client, because he was only fit to be a friend, but not fit for cooperation.

We once gave up a product, because it did nothing except consuming our time.

Sometimes we have to give up some of our companions, because their ambitions and interests are beyond here; —they belong to another fields.

Keyword: Trust

The power of trust can be passed on.

When you trust a person a hundred percent, he won't want to betray you.

Trust is a primary emotion deeply rooted in people's heart that can be mutually infectious.

Even if betrayed, we are still going to infect more people.

Treasure every trust. Speak for CNOOD, and build your own reputation by public praise.

Keyword: Model

A replicable all-win system!

一组特定价值网络的联盟！

供应链管理＋质量管理＋增值服务＋……＝全方位的解决方案

（特点：1. 系统可复制，外界不能复制；2. 联盟在系统复制中，赢得市场优势）

我们需要不断去揣摩理解我们的业务模式，用心地经营我们的模式。

模式可以复制，却又不能完全复制，只有注入我们的心思和心血，才是有血有肉有灵魂的模式，才能让它生生不息。

关键词："流程"

源于客户！
严于客户！
回归客户！

根据客户的执行要求，在经验中总结出适合 CNOOD 的业务流程，持续地完善。

一步步地完善、思考、更新，绝不流于表面。

关键词："归零"

探索、革新、转型是永恒的话题！

志同道合的合伙人不断加入；

合作企业的持续升级；

不间断地组织学习培训成长；

An alliance of specific value networks!

Supply chain management + quality control + value-adding services = a comprehensive solution

(Features: 1. The system is replicable, while the environment is not; 2. The alliance wins market advantage in the system replication.)

We need continually try to understand our business model, and run it with all our heart.

A model can be replicated, but not completely. It can be a model with flesh, soul and undying vitality only if we add hard thinking and painstaking effort to it.

Keyword: Procedure

From the clients!
Stricter than clients!
Back to clients!

According to the clients' requirement of operation, we summarize from experience the working manual that is suited to CNOOD, which is to be further improved.

Step by step, we improve, think about and renew the procedure, never stopping on the surface.

Keyword: Return-to-Zero

Exploration, innovation and transformation are permanent topics.

More and more partners with the same vision;

Continual upgrading of the cooperative companies;

Uninterrupted learning, training and growing;

从贸易走向工程；

从单一产品走向全方位解决方案；

从油气领域，逐步辐射油、气、水、矿山、基建、新能源六大领域。

归零，敢于破釜沉舟，一直创业的路上！

关键词："追梦"

追梦，遥不可及的梦！

去摘，高不可攀的星！

我心中的CNOOD，是一座世外桃源，这里没有博弈，没有尔虞我诈，只需做最真的自己；是一群值得信赖的伙伴，我们互相包容、互相成全、互相成就，一起成长、发展、变老；是一群奋发向上的年轻人，我们怀揣着梦想，期待着创造无限可能的人生；在CNOOD有一群专业的行业大师，我们有太多的选择，亦可享天伦之乐，却更愿意支持CNOOD走向更美好的明天；是老子"无为而治"的实践，是孔孟"仁爱"的布施，是仁义礼智信的倡导，是"善"的最高价值；是你我赖以生存、成长、发展的家园，是你我共同追寻的梦想！

From trade to engineering;

From a single product to comprehensive solutions;

From the area of oil and gas, gradually toward covering six areas including: oil, gas, water, mines, infrastructure construction, and new energies.

Returning to zero and daring burn our boats, we are forever on the way of entrepreneurship.

Keyword: Dream-seeking

Seek the distant, unapproachable dreams!

Reach for the stars high up in the sky!

CNOOD, to my mind, is a Shangri-la where there is neither cunning internal strife nor cheating each other; what we need to do is to be the truest self. It is a group of trustworthy companions, who embrace the spirit of Pristine Simplicity, Amorphous Unity, Reciprocal Constancy, while growing, developing and becoming old together. It is a group of promising, ambitious young people with dreams, who are expecting to create a life with infinite possibilities. In CNOOD we have a group of professional masters of the industry, who have too many choices including enjoying family happiness, and yet prefer to support CNOOD on its way toward a better future. Here you can witness the practice of Laozi's philosophy of "governing by noninterference", the spreading of "benevolence" preached by Confucius and Mencius, the advocacy of traditional moral standards, and the supreme value of "The good". It is the home on which our existence, growth and development depend.

最后，任重道远，感恩我们一起出发，一起探索，一起迎来更美好的 CNOOD。

致诚，致爱，致心！

It is a dream that we all seek!

To conclude, the task is heavy and the way is long. I am grateful that we could start together, explore together, and welcome a better CNOOD together.

The commitment of sincerity, love and heart!

李燕飞
Fay

毕业于上海对外经贸大学，脚踏实地，一步一个脚印走出每一个校园。
2006 年，一句"未来，自己来创造"，开启国际贸易的职业之路。
2012 年，进入 CNOOD，做最真的自己，与伙伴们一起追梦，勇敢地去学习，去探索，去挑战。
生命是一次奇遇，曾以为已拥有很多，仰望星空，才发现真正的旅程才开启。

A graduate from Shanghai University of International Business and Economics, Fay has always been an earnest and down-to-earth person, walking with firm steps out of every campus.
She embarked on a career in the field of international trade in 2006, inspired by the words "I shall create the future myself".
She endeavors to be the truest self and seeks dreams with companions since she joined CNOOD in 2012, while learning, exploring and challenging bravely with them.
Life is an adventure. She used to think that she had already owned a lot, until she looks up at the stars and realizes that the true journey has just begun.

施璐德年鉴（2016）
CNOOD Yearbook (2016)

■ Andy

辞旧迎新，又一年。

蓦然回首，自己来到 CNOOD 已有 5 个年头了，我的身体和灵魂里已有了深深不可磨灭的 CNOOD 烙印。

人生没有彩排，一路走来，有过岔路口，有过辛酸的日子，有过忙碌的日子，有过迷茫的日子，但是我没有放弃，也没有后悔。

我觉得我是一个典型的 CNOOD 人。CNOOD 是一个大家庭，是由你、我、他组成的一个大家庭。也许我们性格迥异，但是我们都是典型的 CNOOD 人。我们构成了 CNOOD 的魂，CNOOD 又塑造了我们的人。

这些年走过很多路，也遇到过很多人，听到过夸奖，也听到过抱怨，不过慢慢都会变成一句话——他是 CNOOD 的

Bidding farewell to the old year, we usher in a new year.

I suddenly realize, when looking back, that I have been working at CNOOD for five years. A deep, indelible mark—a mark of CNOOD—has been stamped both on my soul and my body.

There is no rehearsal in life. When I come all the way along, I have stood at the crossroads, have tasted the bitterness of life, have had busy days, and have experienced confusing times. But I never give up nor regret.

I think I am a typical CNOOD member. CNOOD is a big family, one that is composed of you, him/her and me. We are all typical CNOOD members though we may be of totally different disposition. We make up the soul and spirit of CNOOD, while CNOOD in turn shape our personalities.

I have walked many ways these years, and have met many people; I have heard compliments as well as complaints, which

人，CNOOD 的人都这样。

我觉得 CNOOD 的人出去就代表着认真、较真、负责、守诺、诚信；当然，很多时候也代表着专业。

如果问我，CNOOD 人究竟是什么样的人？我无法给出标准答案，不过我可以说，当你遇到一个 CNOOD 人的时候，你就知道什么是 CNOOD 人。

2016 年的年鉴是 CNOOD 第一次年鉴，我想趁着这个机会分享一下我在 CNOOD 这些年里印象深刻的事情，以及在 CNOOD 的成长。

初来 CNOOD 的第一年是最苦的日子，相比只够支付房租的实习工资，一个人的

gradually turn into one sentence: He is a CNOOD member, and every CNOOD member looks like him.

I believe that a CNNOD member, when in the business world, embodies such qualities as being conscientious, earnest, responsible, true to his word, and in many cases professional, of course.

I am unable to offer a standard answer when asked: What on earth is a CNOOD member? I can say, however, that when you meet a CNOOD member, you will know what a CNOOD member is.

Yearbook 2016 is the first edition of CNOOD Yearbook, and I would like to take the opportunity to share what I find the most impressive as well as my personal development since I joined CNOOD.

My first year in CNOOD was the most difficult time. Compared with the intern

生活其实更难熬。吃饭一个人，生病一个人，搬家一个人，到哪里都是一个人。记得有一次搬家，为了节约5块钱的车费，凌晨一个人在大马路上拖着几件破行李，走走停停。有天晚上突然就哭了，没有缘由，不知道是看了哪篇文章，还是听了哪句歌词，在家里一个人号啕大哭。现在回想起来，那一年的磨砺，也是我人生中最宝贵的财富之一，我的心慢慢沉淀了下来，明白了生活的不易，长大了，也懂事了。

初来上海，寄托着家里的希望，对自己的未来怀着忐忑的心态，不知道未来会怎样，迷茫；记得当时每天上班的穿着就像农民工进城，弯腰驼背，极度的沉默寡言。每天的生活只有工作。但是，其实我对自己第一年的工作态度和工作结果还是挺满意的。我想，如果当时有优秀新人奖，那一定是非我莫属，因为那一年也只有我一个新人。

生活就是这样，我们朝着阳光出发，虽然偶尔会遇到雾霾天、阴雨天，但我心向阳，又有何惧之。

salary that barely covered apartment rental, living alone by myself was even harder to tolerate. I was alone when having meals, when falling ill, when moving house. Wherever I went, I was alone. One morning before dawn, I still remember, I dragged several pieces of shabby luggage along the street, stopping every now and then, only to save five yuan when moving house. One night I began to weep, with no specific reason— maybe because I had read an article, or had heard a sentence of some song. I cried loudly in my apartment, alone. When now I think back, I consider the hardness I went through during that year as one of the most precious wealth in my lifetime. Bit by bit, my mind calms down, and I begin to know that life is not easy. I am growing up, becoming more and more sensible.

When I first came to Shanghai with the hopes of the whole family pinned on me, I was upset and confused about my future, not knowing what was to come. I can still remember those days when I was dressed like a peasant-worker in town, hunchbacked and extremely uncommunicative. There was nothing but work in everyday life, while I was still quite satisfactory about my job attitude and the results of my work. Had there been a "New Employees Award" the year I joined CNOOD, I would definitely have won it since I was the only new employee that year.

This is what life looks like: we set on our journey, facing the sunshine; there is nothing to fear when our hearts embrace the sun, despite the occasional hazy or overcast, rainy days.

每年都会有人说我变得不大一样了，过了几年那是大不一样，有的人说不上具体哪里变得不一样，有的人说我变得自信了，有点人说我变得更成熟了，我觉得我应该是变得越来越像一个 CNOOD 人了，一个更加纯粹的 CNOOD 人。

Every year people tell me that I have changed a little; after several years, that makes a big difference. Some are not sure how specifically I have changed, some say that I have become self-confident, and others say that I am becoming more and more like a CNOOD member, an even purer CNOOD member.

魏坤 / Andy

2012 年初加入 CNOOD，平时喜欢运动，尤其是跑步，现业余时间在上海对外经贸大学攻读 MBA。

Andy joined CNOOD at the beginning of 2012. He likes physical exercises, especially jogging. Now he is pursuing an MBA degree at Shanghai University of International Business and Economics in his spare time.

存至信，一片祥云

Cherish the Utmost Trust, and There Will Come a Propitious Cloud

■ Chemmary

正式加入CNOOD工作近一年，期间惶惶不安，恐无业绩，不能为公司增效；夙夜忧叹，恨无所长，有负公司之信任，唯有兢兢业业、以勤补拙。

多年来，习惯了国企安逸无忧、按部就班的生活，而CNOOD独特的工作氛围、经营理念和公司文化带给了我一个全新的天地。没了日日刷脸的考勤，员工却能够打破固有的作息时间，围绕项目自觉地加班加点；少了天天见面的寒暄，相隔千里之外的人却能够更加畅通、高效的交流和沟通；没了任务性的计划指标，公司业绩却持续突飞猛进；少了程序化的请示汇报，人人却都以主人翁的意识为项目、为公司尽职尽责。所有的这一切，在我看来都源自一个词——信任。

I have been formally working in CNOOD for about one year, during which time I have always been fearful and anxious, worrying that I cannot help improving the company's efficiency. All the time have I lamented my lack of strong ability and been afraid that I might fail to live up to the company's trust. What I can do is to work conscientiously and earnestly, trying to make up my lack of intelligence by diligence.

For many years when I worked in a state-owned enterprise, I was used to the easy, comfortable and programmed way of life, following strictly to prescribed routines. However, CNOOD's unique working atmosphere, business idea and corporate culture have taken me to a totally different world. Without routine attendance checking, people will break old timetable and work willingly overtime for projects. Without daily face-to-face greetings, the communication between people who are thousands of miles away from each other becomes yet easier,

　　加入公司后所做的第一笔订单，是与意大利客户签订的钢管供货合同，对期间的波折记忆犹新。国内钢厂执行预付款排产政策，根据已签订的合同，公司必须预先支付合同定金后钢厂才能进行生产，而意大利客户却因为项目后续制造流程未确定而迟迟无法按合同约定支付预付款，同时还要求我们保证交货期。虽然了解意大利客户内部的实际运作情况，分析断定项目合同是有效的，但取消订单的可能性依然存在。面临客户的预付款未到账和钢厂已排产的矛盾，内心极度迷茫和焦虑，而此时，公司给予了我极大的支持和信任，预先垫付了合同全款，及时完成了第一笔订单的全部生产任务。事后，发货前意大利客户在后续流程确认后承付了全部货款，公司的大力支持促成了后续项目合同的继续签订。

smoother and more effective. Without mandatory planned targets, the company is advancing by leaps and bounds with steadily increasing performance. Without the rigid and inflexible system of reporting, everyone fulfills his/her duty for projects as well as for the company. All these, it seems to me, originate from a single word—"trust".

　　The first order I handled since I joined CNOOD was a steel tube supply contract signed with a client from Italy. Now I can still vividly recall the setbacks I underwent throughout this case. Domestic steelworks adopted a policy that required advance payment before scheduling. Production was to be arranged only after our company had paid the deposit stipulated in the contract. The Italian client, however, acted slowly in terms of the advance payment according to the contract due to the uncertainties in subsequent manufacture process, while insist that we ensure the date of delivery. Though we were clear about the actual status of its internal operations and was sure of the validity of the contract, there still existed the possibility that the Italians should withdraw the order. I was extremely confused and anxious when confronted with the dilemma, when our company gave me great support and trust by paying in advance the total sum of contract, which enabled me to fulfill the manufacture task of my first order ever in CNOOD. Later, the Italian client made the payment of the total sum after the confirmation of subsequent process, prior to the shipment. The powerful support from our company facilitated the signing of contracts for more projects.

信任不是单方面的"赌",是建立在彼此间相互了解的基础上,是在前期长时间的业务合作、交流沟通中逐步建立起来的,是对彼此能力、诚信乃至人性的肯定和升华,是基于实现一个共同梦想产生的心与心的交流。"以金相交,金耗则忘;以利相交,利尽则散;以势相交,势败则倾;以权相交,权失则弃;以情相交,情断则伤;唯以心相交,方能成其久远。"

感谢公司搭建了这个平台,感谢一年来公司和同事们对我的帮助和信任,使我开拓了眼界,增长了知识,也净化了心灵。

我坚信:合伙做事也好,人际交往也好,都应珍惜缘分,珍惜时光。以善为念、以诚相待、以心相交,与高者为伍,与德者同行,存至信,人生必有一片属于你的祥云。

Trust, instead of being a one-sided "gambling", is built on the foundation of mutual understanding. It is gradually built during the previous long-time business cooperation and communication, as mutual affirmation and sublimation of the ability, sincerity and even humanity. It is a heart-to-heart exchange based on the realization of a common dream. "If people make friends out of money, they forget each other when the money is all spent. If people make friends out of interests, they disband when the interests are used up. If people make friends out of influence, the relationship collapses when the influence declines. If people make friends out of power, they abandon each other when the power is lost. If people make friends out of affection, they hurt each other when the affection ceases. Only if people make friends with each other out of heart will the friendship last forever."

I would like to express my gratitude to the company for setting up this platform, and my gratitude to the company as well as to my colleagues for their help and trust, which broadens my horizon, enriches my knowledge and purifies my soul.

I'm of a firm belief, that we should treasure luck and time whether for a partnership or for personal communication. Keep good intentions in mind, treat each other with sincerity, and make friends out of heart. Always be with the noble, and walk with the virtuous. Cherish the utmost trust, and there must be a propitious cloud for you.

吕秀丽
Chemmary

吕秀丽，女，1969年9月出生，山东烟台人，经济管理专业学士毕业。在国有钢铁企业先后从事财会、统计、管理等工作，此后专注于外贸业务近十余载，熟知外贸业务流程、出口单证、物流等各项业务。信守"敏而好学，勤能补拙"，并在实际业务之中得以体现和运用。

Born in September 1969, Chemmary is from Yantai, Shandong Province. She received a bachelor's degree in Economic Management. After doing various jobs including accounting, statistics and management in a state-owned steel company, she has been specializing in export business for nearly ten years, familiar with international trade procedures, export documentation and logistics. She firmly believes the old teaching that is embodied and employed in her daily work:"Be quick-minded and eager to learn; make up your lack of intelligence by diligence."

来过 CNOOD
I Have Been in CNOOD

■ Connor

2014 年 11 月 20 日，我参加了 CNOOD 在上海大学延长校区的宣讲会，参与宣讲的人有 Dennis、Tina Xu、Roger、Jane、Queeny。

2014 年 12 月 8 日收到了 CNOOD 的 offer。2015 年 1 月 5 日在 CNOOD 开始实习工作。

2015 年 1 月末的年会上，与 Lilia、Sissi 一起合演无声哑剧，与 Tracy、Adalind 一起登台表演 F(x) 的舞蹈。

2015 年 3 月开始在 CNOOD 的培训课程，2015 年 3 月 18 日，选定 Loreen 为自己的带教师父。

2015 年 4 月，跟随 CNOOD 的同事们去巴厘岛春游，是人生中第一次出国旅游的经历。

2015 年 5 月 2 日，来到常熟，和 Loreen、Chris、Jenna、Sissi 一起开始

On November 20, 2014, I took part in CNOOD's recruitment activity held in Shanghai University (Yanchang Campus). Among the CNOOD members attending the activity were Dennis, Tina Xu, Roger, Jane and Queeny.

On December 8, 2014, I received an offer from CNOOD. From February 5, 2015, I began my internship in CNOOD.

On the annual meeting at the end of February 2015, I performed mime with Lilia and Sissi, and performed a dance of *F(x)*, a girls group of popular music from Korea, with Tracy and Adalind.

In March 2015, I started my training course in CNOOD. On March 18, 2015, I chose Loreen as my tutor.

In April 2015, I went on a spring outing to Bali Island with fellow staff members in CNOOD, as my first experience of travelling abroad.

On May 2, 2015, I came to Changshu with Loreen, Chris, Jenna and Sissi, to start

参与常熟工厂的建厂工作。采购设备,安排人员,现场勘查,整体规划……在忙碌而艰难中前行。

2015年6月,常熟工厂第一批货物装船。

2015年8月,常熟工厂第三船货物装船,第一个项目圆满完成。

2015年11月,在合肥紫金钢管股份有限公司完成第一次独立跟单。

2015年12月,第一个4 300吨的澳洲项目下单。期间,BSW、Sanhe和CNOOD(常熟)均经历了多种磨难。为

the construction of Changshu Processing Center. Equipment procurement, staffing, on-the-spot survey, and overall planning … We made progress during a busy and difficult time.

In June 2015, the shipment of the first batch of goods from Changshu Processing Center was finished.

In August 2015, with the shipment of the third batch of goods from Changshu Processing Center, the first project was successfully completed.

In November 2015, I handled an order independently for the first time, with Hefei Ziking Steel Pipe CO., LTD.

In December 2015, we received the order of 4,300 tons from the first Australian project. Afterwards, BSW, Sanhe and

了一句属于 CNOOD 的承诺，我们最终在 2016 年 4 月 10 日前将货物备妥。2016 年 4 月 20 号，货物开始装船，4 月 23 日，装船结束。2016 年 5 月 18 日，收到 Worley Parsons 的邮件，第一根海桩管打桩完毕。

2016 年 4 月 30 日—2016 年 5 月 2 日，与 Dennis、Fay、Pat、Andy 以及上海对外经贸大学的 MBA 同学一起参加于阿拉善盟腾格里沙漠举办的"亚沙赛"（即"亚太地区商学院沙漠挑战赛"），3 天 76 公里的行程，修身修心修灵。

2016 年 5 月 27 日，收到第二个澳洲项目的 PO。2016 年 9 月 16 日，第二个澳洲项目在常熟装船结束。

2016 年 10 月，加入 Paul Chen 的项目团队。

2016 年 12 月 13 日—2017 年 1 月 23 日，澳洲 Amrun 项目，在 PCK 协助 J. Steel 进行项目管理。一年之内第三次接手澳洲项目，往事种种，历历在目。

从未想过，自己在工作的前两年，能有如此多的机会与经历，也从未想过能如此有幸，和这么多有趣的人做这么多有趣的事。也许在未来的某一瞬间，回头看看这份年鉴，看到某一行潦草的文字，回忆

CNOOD Changshu all went through various hardships. Keeping a promise made by CNOOD, we finally got the goods ready before April 10, 2016. The shipment began on April 20 and finished on April 23. On May 18, 2016, we received an e-mail from Worley Parsons informing us that the piling of the first marine pile pipe was completed.

Between April 30 and May 2, 2016, Dennis, Fay, Pat, Andy and I, together with MBA candidates from Shanghai University of International Business and Economics, entered for the Asian-Pacific Business Schools Desert Challenge. We covered seventy-six kilometers in three days across the Tengger Desert, Alxa (Alashan) League. It was a cultivation of the body, the mind as well as the soul.

On May 27, 2016, we received the OP from the second Australian project. On September 16, 2016, the shipment of goods for the second Australian project was finished in Changshu.

In October 2016, I joined the project team led by Paul Chen.

Between December 13, 2016 and February 23, 2017, I assisted J. Steel in project management at PCK for the Amrun project. It was the third time I took over an Australian project in one single year. I still vividly remember many things that happened at that time.

Before I joined CNOOD, I had never imagined that I would have so many opportunities and experiences in the first two years of working, and that I should be so lucky to do so many interesting things

起那一段同甘共苦的岁月，会有万丈的豪情；看到像素不高的照片，回忆起那台湾的卤肉饭，会有家的温馨；听到那熟悉的音乐，回忆起上海滩的风起云涌，会有更加坚定的信念，走好以后的每一步路。

with so many interesting people. Maybe in a particular moment many years later, when I read this yearbook again, I will be filled with pride and enthusiasm at the sight of a line of hasty, careless handwriting, recalling the time when we shared joys and sorrows; when I see a blurred photo, the remembrance of the Taiwan-style stewed meat rice will remind me of the sweetness of home; when I hear a familiar piece of music, the dynamic and exciting life in the big city of Shanghai will be brought to mind, reinforcing my belief to walk firmly, step by step, in the way ahead.

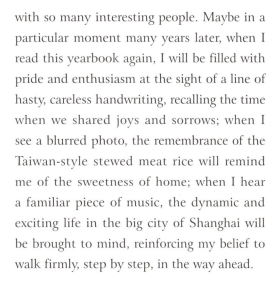

林焕
Connor

1992 年 3 月 13 日，出生于浙江省宁波市。
1999—2005 年就读于宁波市江东中心小学，期间连续 2 年获得宁波市江东区小学生排球比赛冠军。
2005—2008 年就读于宁波市兴宁中学。
2008—2011 年就读于浙江省宁波中学。
2011—2015 年就读于上海大学。
2015 年 1 月 5 日，进入 CNOOD 实习。
2015 年 6 月毕业于上海大学，学士学位，上海市优秀毕业生。
2015 年 7 月 1 日，正式入职 CNOOD。
2016 年 4 月 30 日—5 月 2 日，参加第 5 届"亚沙赛"。

He was born in Ningbo, Zhejiang Province on March 13, 1992.
He attended Ningbo Jiangdong Central Primary School from 1999 to 2005, during which time he won the primary-school volleyball championship of Jiangdong District, Ningbo City for two consecutive years.
He attended Ningbo Xingning Middle School from 2005 to 2008.
He attended Ningbo High School, Zhejiang Province from 2008 to 2011.
He studied at Shanghai University from 2011 to 2015.
He began his internship in CNOOD from January 5, 2015.
He graduated from Shanghai University with a bachelor's degree in June 2015 as an "Outstanding Graduate of Shanghai".
He formally joined CNOOD on July 1, 2015.
He took part in the Fifth Asian-Pacific Business Schools Desert Challenge during April 30 to May 2, 2016.

我眼中的施璐德

What I know about CNOOD

■ Cristhian Allende

当我加入施璐德时,没有想到这家公司秉持了跟大企业一样的高标准,却并未失去中小企业特有的灵活性。施璐德的标准和工具(比如 Workbench)达到了世界水平,与此同时又很注重增进全体员工之间的良好关系,消除职位高低带来的地位差别;此外,鼓励员工家人参与公司各项活动,培养员工的家庭观念,使大家能够互相关心、共同分享,造福全体施璐德人。这样的公司文化使施璐德取得了可喜的业绩,整个团队积极性高涨,并致力于探索新的发展路径。我坚信:只要沿着这条道路前进,施璐德必将在今后数年内大放异彩。

我个人的座右铭是"保持微笑,与人为善,感恩他人"。我的目标是用自己的技能服务于公司的任何一个人,不仅是为公司作贡献,而且也是为大家的个人发展提供帮助。

When I joined CNOOD I never imagined that this company had standards as high as the big corporations, but without losing the agility that characterizes the small and medium-sized enterprises. CNOOD has world-class standards and tools, such as the Workbench, but also promotes healthy relationships among all of its employees, without any distinction by position; also integrates the employee's family to the activities of the company and cultivates Family Values, where all the members care and share each other, ensuring the well-being of all of them. This culture has helped to CNOOD to get great achievements, having a self-motivated team and searching for new ways of development. I am sure that CNOOD on this path will be very successful in the coming years.

Under my personal motto "smile, be nice and says thanks", my goal is offer my skills to anybody in the organization to help not only to the company, also to our people in their individual developments.

Cristhian has worked in more than 10 countries and lived for more than 1 year in 3. He likes to play football, he thinks about himself is a great striker, and also goes to the gym 3 times per week. When he was young practiced different sports: rugby, baseball, tennis, basketball. In his entire working life he has never rejected to take participation in any new project, he strong believes that learning different matters, and doing different jobs, one will be a more rounded person, at professional and personal level. For the same reason, when have some free-time, try to read a book, at least read some news … He has a Psychology's book that haven't being able to read from 10 year ago (never enough calm/peace time to read such kind of book) … he believes one day will do it …

Cristhian is a person who makes decisions based on information plus instinct and expertise … you will never will get all the information requested to make a decision, therefore must trust in yourself, in your capabilities. He is an easy-going person, is able to have fun with their workmates after working hours, and being professional and focus on the job during the working hours, doesn't mix up the relationships. He frequently is smiling, in despite when he was a young boy his father warned to him not smile too much because the people will take advantage of that one, "they will fool you", his father said.

Cristhian would like to know who was the creator of the mankind and who created to the Creator … he believes in Jesus, but also is interested about Buddha and other religions, as well as he believes in Aliens and life in other planets … has a hodgepodge in his mind but it doesn't disturb to him, by the contrary, he is working on finding the common thread to this one … maybe in his afterlife this job will be finished.

Last, but not least, Cristhian has 4 kids, the first one from his first marriage and the other three from the second one, theirs names are Nicolas, Abril, Baltazar and Lola (in the same order), His wife is Ana, he loves a lot her because helps to Cristhian to be a better person, she is much better than him.

启 程
Starting on a New Journey

■ Dannie

人生就像一盒巧克力，你永远不知道下一块会是什么味道。正是因为这种不确定性，我们才对未来充满期待。不过，未来也掌握在自己的手中。一路跌跌撞撞，一路蜿蜒前行，只要坚持不懈，终会到达胜利的彼岸。所以说，未来既是未知的又是已知的。

如果把人生比作一段旅程，那么我已扬帆起航。2016年是充满挑战的一年，加入一个陌生的环境，在相互关心、创造开心的氛围中融入、成长。学会做一个有思想的人，通过对目标的分解以逐个击破，达成终极目标。结识一群志同道合的有梦想的小伙伴，在相互激励、学习中共同进步。第一次在公司庆生，感受爱与关怀。第一次出差，考验细腻心思与规划安排。把握发展的方向，在不同的领域里拓展自己的眼界和能力。建立新的部门，熟悉独立工作与团队协作。自我认识和学习，通过书本和交流促进智商和情商等多方面的能力提升。把工作分解成一个个任务，在

Life is like a box of chocolates; you never know what you're going to get. In fact, we feel hopeful about the future just because of this uncertainty. However, the future is also in our hands. We've come all the way along, stumbling and wriggling, and are sure to reach the destination so long as we are persistent. Therefore, to us the future is unknown and known at the same time.

If life is compared to a journey, I've already set forth on it. The year 2016 was one full of challenge, when I entered an unfamiliar environment, mixing and growing in an atmosphere of caring for each other and creating delightfulness. I tried to be a person of thought, reaching the goal by breaking it down into sub-goals and solving them one by one. I got to know a group of fellow staff members with dreams who shared the same aspiration and purpose, making progress together by mutual encouragement and learning. For the first time in life I celebrated my birthday in the company,

任务执行中学会总结和反思，积累经验，避免曲折。团队建设，在春游、秋游等集体活动中增强凝聚力，培养团队精神。两次年会，在泪水中感动，树立一颗更加坚定的前进的心。

2017年，我期待乘风破浪。我明白通往成功的路从来不会一帆风顺，我时刻准备着，迎接新的挑战与历练。2017年，我与CNOOD同行。

附上2016级小伙伴合影，愿时光不老，我们不散。

feeling the caring love. My first business trip was a test of my thoughtfulness and scheduling ability. I learned how to capture the trends of development, broadening my horizon and expanding my capabilities in various fields. Through setting up a new department, I accustomed myself to working independently as well as cooperating with other group members. As for self-cognition and self-learning, I promoted my competences in different dimensions, intelligently and emotionally alike, through reading and personal communication. Decomposing the job into smaller assignments, I learned to summarize and reflect on my work, accumulated experiences and avoided twists and turns, in the process of fulfilling these assignments. As for team building, I enhanced the cohesion with other members of the organization and cultivated my team spirit by participating in group activities such as spring and autumn outings. I was moved into tears during the two annual meetings I took part in, and was since then more determined to make further progress.

I wish I could go ahead braving all hardships in 2017. I'm fully aware that the way to success is never smooth. In every moment, I'm ready for new challenges and trials. In 2017, I shall continue the journey with CNOOD.

Below is a photo of fellow staff members who joined CNOOD in 2016. I wish that time stopped passing, and that we never separated.

VISION DRIVEN LIFE-CNOOD 2008 TO 2016

徐丹妮
Dannie

年龄：保密
星座：最聚财的大金牛
学校：佛罗里达大学
愿景：充实的精神世界 + 逛吃逛吃的生活
兴趣：安静地待着，偶有雅兴，留些许文字抒怀

Penname: Dannie
Age: Secret
Zodiac Sign: Taurus, the most capable of gathering money
Alma Mater: University of Florida
Vision: A rich mental world plus shopping and eating
Interest: Staying quietly, and expressing my feelings with a few words occasionally if in a poetic mood

2016 年年鉴

■ Eric

年年岁岁花相似，岁岁年年人不同。时间过得飞快，年龄的增长是否就伴随着成长？有些人少年老成，有些人活得依然如老顽童。时间给了我无数次的机会去磨砺，我是成长了？还是只是被生活磨去当年意气风发，年少轻狂？

每一句话都会可能成为的你人生的注脚，或是智慧，或是无知，或是沉稳，或是浮躁。让思想快速前行，但减少自己的言语。这是为了一语中的，是为了节约他人的宝贵时间。我希望自己也能如前人般指点江山，挥斥方遒；希望如前辈般张弛有度，宠辱不惊；希望如前行者般静如处子，动若脱兔。积累会在谈吐中体现，新一年愿谨言慎行，优雅如新。

"Year after year, flowers look similar; year after year, people are changing." Time flies, but are we really growing up when we are older in age? Some people are young but mature, while others are old but behave like innocent children. As days are passing quickly, I have been given numerous opportunities for cultivating myself. Am I growing up? Or is it only that the youthful craziness is rubbed off form me by the coarseness of life?

Any words you say might become a footnote to your life—wisdom or ignorance, reliability or flippancy. Let the thought in your mind go fast, but slow down your speech, so that you hits home with a single remark, saving the valuable time of others. I wish I could, like the forefathers and my predecessors, remark on public affairs in a bold and unstrained manner; know the extent of tension and relaxation, indifferent to personal gains and losses; and know when to take proper action. One's experience will be reflected in his speech. I wish I would be

2016 年，也是我情感成长的一年。生活总会给你开一些让你无法接受的玩笑，令你愤怒、无助、失望、痛苦。感谢我有着坚强的后盾，我的家人、朋友、公司，让我鼓足了力量，砥砺前行。总说家是港湾，贪图于享受湾里的平静与包容。外出的征程，带着一身尘土，回家落座，总有家的味道与温暖，却任港湾承受风雨交加，伤痕累累。港湾是需要经营与修葺的。付出需要理解，支持需要感谢，不安需要安慰，哭泣需要抚去眼角的泪痕，互相包容，你也是它的港湾，一起历经风雨感动，感谢所有！

more cautious in both word and action, as a new, graceful person.

The year 2016 also witnessed my emotional growth. Life will always make jokes that you are unable to accept; you will be angry, feel helpless, be disappointed, and feel pains. I'm grateful that I have strong support from my family, friends and CNOOD, who have encouraged me to summon up strength and move on through hardships. We say that home is a harbor, and we all indulge in its calmness and forgivingness. When we return home and get seated, covered with dust from a journey, we always feel its smell and warmth. However, we often leave the harbor to strong storms, making it scarred all over. A harbor needs maintenance and renovation. When one makes sacrifice, he needs understanding; when one supports you, he needs thanks; when one is uneasy, he needs consolation; when one weeps, he needs you to wipe away the tear stains around his eyes. Embrace your home while it embraces you, because you are the harbor for it as it is a harbor for you. Together will you and your home go through winds and rains, with gratitude to all!

许益源
Eric

作者于 2013 年毕业，因 Dennis 亲自倒的一杯水，有感于公司平等、尊重的文化风格，遂入 CNOOD 之大平台。几年间，经历了许多事情，虽远不及成熟，但亦意识到自己的成长。三十而立之期即将来临，目标远大，前路漫漫，当不断前行。

Moved by its corporate culture of equality and respect, reflected in a cup of water poured by Dennis himself, Eric joined the big platform of CNOOD after graduating from college. He has since then gone through many things and he can feel his own growth, though still far from being mature. He'll soon be 30 years old. His goal is high, yet the way is long. He has to make steady progress.

施璐德亚洲有限公司董事长候选人申请
Applying for Candidacy for Chairman of Board of CNOOD ASIA LIMITED

■ Dennis

各位董事：

我郑重申请施璐德亚洲有限公司董事长候选人资格。

作为施璐德亚洲有限公司的一员，作为施璐德亚洲有限公司董事会成员：

1. 我有为公司服务的强烈意愿；
2. 我有为股东服务的强烈意愿；
3. 我有为董事会服务的强烈意愿；
4. 如果有幸被选为施璐德亚洲有限公司董事长，我有带领董事会全面支持、配合和落实公司CEO各项工作的强烈意愿。

我充分明白，不管是什么岗位，在施璐德，都是一个为公司服务的机会，而不是一个职位、一个官僚。

我充分明白，施璐德亚洲有限公司董事长的年薪为一元人民币。

我充分明白，施璐德亚洲有限公司董事长必须做业务，做好业务，必须在各方面做出表率，并接受监督。

Distinguished directors of board,

I now solemnly apply for the candidacy for chairman of CNOOD ASIA LIMITED.

As a member of CNOOD ASIA LIMITED, and also as a member of its board of directors, I am of strong aspiration

1. to serve the company;
2. to serve the shareholders;
3. to serve board of directors; and
4. to lead board of directors to support, coordinate and fulfill the works of CEO in all areas, if I am lucky enough to be elected the chairman of CNOOD ASIA LIMITED.

I am fully aware, that whatever post one takes in CNOOD means an opportunity to serve the company, not a title or rank.

I am fully aware, that the salary for chairman of CNOOD ASIA LIMITED is RMB one yuan.

I am fully aware, that anyone who acts as chairman of CNOOD ASIA LIMITED must be engaged in business and be successful, set examples in all aspects, while in the meantime

我充分明白，本届施璐德亚洲有限公司董事长的任期将随本届董事会任期的结束而结束。

请各位董事给予我一个机会，投出您神圣的一票。

being supervised.

I am fully aware, that the tenure of office of chairman of CNOOD ASIA LIMITED lasts as long as that of board of directors.

I hereby ask every director of board to cast your solemn vote and give me this opportunity.

施璐德亚洲有限公司 CEO 候选人推荐函

各位股东，各位同事，各位董事：

经过8年多考察，通过对多位候选人观察，郑重推荐李燕飞女士作为施璐德亚洲有限公司的CEO候选人。主要考虑如下：

李燕飞女士从善如流，仁心拳拳。对待国内外同事，一视同仁，注重解决问题，从不与同事恶意争执；对待客户，如同家人，从不与客户争斗。在市场上，在同事中，赢得广泛赞誉；为公司树立良好市场形象，建立良好口碑。

她始终坚持，勤奋好学。学业方面，MBA毕业论文，初获好评；教育论坛，创新演讲，论点突出，获得认可；求学不倦，勤奋阅读，诸子百家，古今中外，广泛涉猎；游学不止，学术交流，勤勉不断。

她大公无私，严于律己。200万善款，赋予公司，年会春游，从不宣扬；提成分配，从不相争；客户授予，客观透明。律己从严，待人从宽，实事求是，公正客观。积极做事，诲人不倦。

她勤于锻炼，善于养生。思想积极，身康体健。

基于此，特郑重推荐李燕飞女士作为施璐德亚洲有限公司的CEO候选人，相信她会带领大家从一个成功迈向又一个成功。

执行董事：池勇海

2017/1/5

Recommendation Letter

Having observed several candidates for more than eight years, I solemnly recommend Li Yanfei (Fay) as the candidate for CEO of CNOOD ASIA LIMITED, based on following considerations:

As a kindhearted person, she is always ready to accept good advice. She treats colleagues from home and abroad equally without discrimination. She gives priority to problem solving, never disputing with colleagues with malice. As with clients, she treats them as family members and never has strife with them. She has been widely acclaimed in the market as well as among fellow workers. She has contributed to the establishment of good image and reputation for our company.

She persists in her study with diligence and eagerness. For starters, her MBA dissertation received favorable comments. Her innovative speech given on the educational forum was well received for its outstanding argument. Out of an untiring pursuit of knowledge, she was well read in various fields and topics, covering a wide range of classic works. Assiduously, she travels a lot through academic exchanges.

She is a selfless person of self-discipline. She has donated two million yuan to sponsor the company's annual meetings, never advertizing it. She never argues about her percentage. She maintains impartiality and transparency in distributing client resources within the company. She is strict with herself and lenient towards others. In daily work, she adopts a practical and realistic approach based on facts, sticking to the principles of objectivity and impartiality. She is active in doing things, and tireless in teaching subordinates.

With the habit of physical exercises, she excels in maintaining good health. While being perfectly healthy, she is of active mentality, too.

I hereby solemnly recommend Li Yanfei (Fay) as the candidate for CEO of CNOOD ASIA LIMITED, in the belief that the company, with her leadership, will march from victory to victory.

Executive Director
Dennis Chi
January 15, 2017

Carta de Referencia

Estimados miembros de la Junta, compañeros y directores:

Después de haber supervisado a varios candidatos en los últimos ocho años, les recomiendo aquí solemnemente la señora Li Yanfei (Faylee) como candidata para la elección CEO de CNOOD ASIA LIMITED, teniendo en consideración los siguientes aspectos:

Con el corazón lleno de bondad, Faylee siempre ha tratado los compañeros con imparcialidad tanto a los colegas chinos como a los de otros países. Durante su trabajo diario, siempre da prioridad a la solución de problemas, así que nunca discute con sus compañeros con mala intención. Cuando comunica con los clientes, les trata con tanta amabilidad como si fueran su propia familia. En el mercado, ha recibido ampliamente alabanzas de los homólogos de esta industria. Con todo estos resfuerzos, ha contribuido establecer una buena imagen y la reputación honrada para nuestra empresa.

Con respecto a los estudios, insiste mejorar sus conocimientos constantemente. A lo largo de su curso MBA, ha recibido muy buenos comentarios sobre su trabajo académico; Por otro lado, ha ganado reconocimiento por el Foro de Educación, una propuesta muy inovadora suya. Aparte de los cursos académicos, he observado también su gran pasión en leer una amplia especie de obras: sus interés pasa desde los libros clásicos de nuestro pasado chino, hasta los pensadores destacados del mundo occidental, así recibe la nutrición de ideas de las cien escuelas de pensamiento. Gracias a su diligencia y las cualidades inatas, ella está en un camino de mejoramiento en sí misma sin cesar.

Ha mostrado su imparcialidad y altruismo con las prácticas auténticas: ha donado cantidad de dinero como patrocinador del viaje anual de la empresa sin importar su propio interés. Recibe su parte de retribución de manera modesta y atribuye recursos con transparencia. Como una persona de autodisciplina, ella sin embargo, trata a los demás con mucha tolerancia. Con los méritos de imparcialidad y objetividad, Faylee siempre ha comportado como una optimista e impartido sus conocimientos a los alumnos sin reserva.

Y por último, tiene costumbre de hacer ejercicios físicos con el fin de mantener buena condición de salud, así como una base firme para dedicarse con vigor a su carrera profesional.

Basando en todos los aspectos mencionados, me es grato recomendar aquíla señora Li Yanfei(Faylee) como candidata para la elección de CEO de CNOOD ASIA LIMITED, convencido de que con su liderazgo, nuestra empresa tendrá un futuro lleno de éxitos y prosperidad.

Director Ejecutivo
Dennis Chi
Fecha: 2017/1/5

池勇海，男，汉族，1970年出生于湖北仙桃。先后毕业于武汉理工大学、复旦大学，获管理学硕士学位、经济学博士学位。

他是一名跨国公司的创立人、执行董事。他致力于构筑一个平台，打造一个共创、共享、共治的无边界的有机生态系统。让每一位在这个平台上的国内外合伙人、员工都能在这里成长、壮大成为未来的CEO。

他也是一个"屌丝"，上演了一场真正的屌丝逆袭。从农村里走出来的孩子，羞涩，不自信，哑巴英语到国际谈判中的从容、睿智、优雅的转身。

他是一个造梦者，他告诉身边的每一个人，无论你是想做一个业界精英、老板CEO或是哲学家、诗人、乞丐都可以。心有多远，你就能走多远！

他更是一个履梦人，为了实现自己的"中国梦"，先后造访了乌克兰、德国、伊朗、叙利亚、印度尼西亚、智利、澳大利亚、伊拉克、美国、土耳其、厄瓜多尔、尼日利亚、印度、埃及、沙特、巴拿马、玻利维亚等数十个国家。他用他的双脚丈量着世界，也用他的梦想为中国制造与中国创造走向世界贡献自己的力量。

池勇海
Dennis

Born in Xiantao, Hubei Province in 1970, Dennis Chi is of Han nationality and graduated from Wuhan University of Technology with a master's degree in Management Science and from Fudan University with a doctoral degree in Economics.

He is the founder and executive director of a multinational company, devoting himself to building a platform and an organic ecosystem without boundary, which is created, shared and managed by all its members, so that every partner, domestic or foreign, as well as every employee, can grow stronger to become a future CEO.

He used to be a "loser"; however, he performed a real counterattack. Once a shy, unconfident boy from the countryside with extremely poor English speaking proficiency, he has transformed into a business leader who shows calmness, wisdom and grace in international negotiations.

He is a dream-maker who tells everyone around him: "You could be any kind of person, be it professional elite, boss, CEO, or be it philosopher, poet, and beggar— whatever. You can go as far as your heart goes!"

He is also a dream-fulfiller who, in order to realize his "Chinese Dream", has visited dozens of countries: Ukraine, Germany, Iran, Syria, Indonesia, Chile, Australia, Iraq, USA, Turkey, Ecuador, Nigeria, India, Egypt, Saudi Arabia, Panama, Bolivia, etc. He measures the world with his feet, and with his dreams he makes contribution to pushing Chinese manufacture and Chinese creation to the world.

CEO 就职演讲
CEO Inaugural Speech

■ Fay

尊敬的赵总,尊敬的章总,尊敬的杨总,各位朋友、同事、女士们、先生们:

下午好!

曾经问过老池,而且不是一次,"你对每个人的好,都是真的吗?"

他回答:"即便是装的,装一辈子,还需要问真的还是假的吗?"

CNOOD 对合作伙伴,如同一家人。

互相关心,创造开心,已经成为每一个 CNOOD 人心中的印记,以爱互信,上善若水,这份真心实意的关爱让我们成为同舟共济的一辈子的伙伴、朋友、家人。

工作十一年多,带团队也有近十年了,有时候,我觉得我可以帮助他们成长,做事,协助解决实际问题。

Distinguished Mr. Zhao, Mr. Zhang, Mr. Yang, Dear friends, my colleagues, ladies and gentlemen,

Good afternoon.

I have asked Dennis, more than once: "Is your kindness toward everyone genuine?"

His reply: "Maybe it is pretended. But do we need to ask whether it is genuine or pretended if I pretended to be kind through my lifetime?"

For its cooperative partners, CNOOD is like a family.

Caring numbers of others' delightfulness, creating new ocean of delightfulness—this has become a mark on every CNOOD member's heart. Mutual trust with love, and the supreme goodwill that resembles the nature of water—This whole-hearted caring love make us lifelong companions, friends, and family.

After working for more than eleven years and leading teams for nearly ten years, sometimes I believe that I could help them to grow, work and solve practical problems.

但是，想要成为真正的导师，更要在思想上引导他们，帮助他们实现自我。

但老池说："只要真心为他们好。"

我只要用心陪伴他们成长就好，帮助他们做最好的自己就好，其他的部分：无论是不同专业领域的指导，还是思想困惑的引导，会有更多的人一起做。因为这里不仅有许多杰出的人，更重要的是大家都愿意培养人，帮助人，关心人。上善若水，厚德载物。Ben 给我们分享易经、国学；Dennis 引导我们跟随内心；Amir 带领我们做 EPC；Paul 引领我们走向业主；Pat 让我们知道如何做一个上善若水的知性女子；Tina 带我们开拓新能源。这里的每个人，都身藏绝技，在一起，有什么理由胆怯，大踏步往前走就好了。

However, to be a real mentor means more than that;—I must guide them mentally, helping them to realize the true self.

But Dennis said, "If you're truly doing things to their benefit, that's enough."

All that I need to do is to be with them whole-heartedly when they grow up, and to help them to be the best. The remaining part, whether the instructions in different professions or the guidance in clearing up mental perplexity, will be done by a lot more people, not only because we have a galaxy of talent but also because everyone here is willing to nurture, help and care for others. The supreme goodwill resembles the nature of water, which benefits all beings and yet does not contend with anyone; a person with great virtue can take on greater responsibilities. Ben shares with us the wisdom of *Books of Changes* and other traditional learning of China; Dennis teaches us to follow the heart; Amir guides us to carry out EPC; Paul takes us to be closer to owners; Pat lets us know how to

所以，自我们成为 CNOOD 人的那一刻，这里的每一件事情，都是我们共同的事情。

这里没有"该不该我做的事"，我们所有人都已经全权受权参与公司的方方面面，我们培养的是综合型 CEO，我们都是 CEO。

这里也没有"我没把握做的事"，只要敢想，想做，我们所有人都会得到同事和公司全力的支持，我们身后的团队无所不能。

在过去几年，我脑子里只想着如何填补同事们所需要的工作，而同事们对我的包容、信任、支持，也鼓励并帮助我完成了一个又一个"我与 CNOOD 的第一次"，这些涉及业务发展，人力资源，技术质量，组织宣传：

1）CNOOD 第一场校园宣讲会（上海对外经贸大学——我的母校），当然，也是我的第一次校园宣讲演讲，自此，我们开启了一年一季的名校宣讲会，迎来一批又一批优秀的储备人才；

be an intelligent woman with the supreme goodwill; Tina leads us to explore new energies: everyone here has his/her unique expertise. Is there any reason to be timid when we are together? Just stride forward. That's enough.

Therefore, every business here is our common concern ever since the moment we became CNOOD members.

In CNOOD, there isn't anything that we would ask ourselves:"Should I do it or not?" All of us have been fully authorized to participate in every aspect of the company. What we aim to train are synthetic CEOs;—we are all CEOs.

In CNOOD, there isn't anything that we would say:"I'm not sure whether I can do it or not." We will be fully supported by our colleagues and the company if we have the courage of imagination and the desire of achieving something, because we have an omnipotent team behind us.

During the past years, I have been always thinking about how to fill up the work needed by my colleagues. Their forgiveness, trust and support, in turn, have encouraged and helped me to realize many a "first time for CNOOD and me", covering various areas including business development, human resources, technology and quality control, organizing and publicity:

1) CNOOD's first campus recruitment activity (in Shanghai University of International Business and Economics, my Alma Mater), and my first campus recruitment speech of course, after which we held campus recruitment activities in top universities

2）CNOOD第一次春游（武夷山——我的家乡），然后我们的足迹一起探游云南、桂林、巴厘岛、杭州、乌镇、溧阳等；

3）CNOOD第一份与TUV的长协，并逐步有了稳定的第三方检验伙伴，为我们质量管理提供专业的技术指导与把控；

4）CNOOD第一份业务执行操作手册定稿，并将操作手册延伸到不同工作模块如投标、结算、质量检验等，这样，CNOOD的每一位同事，都能通过学习得到详细的操作指引；

and colleges on an annual basis, acquiring excellent talent reserves.

2) CNOOD's first spring outing (in Wuyi Mountain, my hometown), after which we have left our footprints in Yunnan, Guilin, the Bali Island, Hangzhou, Wuzhen, Liyang etc.

3) CNOOD's first long-term agreement with TUV, after which we have gradually developed steady TPI partners, providing professional technical guidance and control for our quality management.

4) The finalization of CNOOD's first Work-manual for business operation, and its extension to various segments such as tendering, settlement, quality control etc., by which every member in CNOOD could get detailed direction through learning.

5）CNOOD 第一版的质量管理体系，逐步发现人才并建立属于 CNOOD 的技术质量部门；

6）CNOOD 丰富的宣传册设计与 PPT 展示；

7）曾经认为出差两周是我的极限，但一次次刷新飞行纪录，为的是让更多的人认识 CNOOD，见证我们的坚持，并通过合作逐步成为中国制造的 fans；

……

一步步走来，我越来越意识到，我们

5) CNOOD's first version of quality control system, by which we have gradually found talented employees and established CNOOD's own technology and quality control departments.

6) The design and enrichment of CNOOD's publicity brochure, and PPT presentations.

7) The records of the flying time on business trip broken repeatedly by me, who used to believe that two weeks was the limit to the time of business trip, only to let more people know CNOOD, witness our perseverance and gradually become fans of Chinese manufacturing through cooperation.

...

With my steps along the way here, I

正在建立一个家一样的归宿,在这里,有一群彼此信任的伙伴,这里有一群勤恳上进的年轻人,亦有一群专业的行业大师,我们只要做最真的自己,勇敢前行,迎来全新的更强的自己。

感恩,我们共同努力的每一天,我来到施璐德的这些年,见证并且参与了施璐德的所有变化:

1)合伙人团队更加完善,全球分公司和市场的布局越来越全面;

2)项目管理流程的持续完善,研发、启用、升级 Workbench;

3)石油、天然气、水、矿山、基建、新能源领域的 EPC 项目的探索、成长、发展;

4)质量管理体系的建立得越来越健全;

5)商业模式的升级转型;

6)投融资部门、人力资源部门的新建,公司内各部门搭建越来越合理;

7)建立 CNOOD 海桩管制造中心和钢结构制造中心。

……

作为一个持续成长转型的公司,我们有很多与 CNOOD 共同成长的机会。

get an increasing stronger feeling that we are building a home to return to, where we have companions who trust each other, young people who work diligently and make progress, and professional gurus in the industry. What we need to do is to be the truest self and advance bravely, embracing a brand-new, stronger self.

I am grateful to every day of us making effort together. During the years since I came to CNOOD, I have witnessed and participated in all its changes:

1) The team of partners has been improved, and the global distribution of branch companies and markets are becoming more and more comprehensive;

2) The continual improvement of project management process, and the R&D, launching and upgrading of Workbench;

3) The exploration, growing and development of EPC projects in the fields of oil, gas, water, mines, infrastructure construction and new energies.

4) Quality control system is being perfected;

5) The business model is going through upgrading and transformation;

6) With the newly established departments of investment and financing as well as human resources, the structure of departments within the company are being rationalized;

7) CNOOD manufacturing center for marine pile pipes and steel structures has been set up.

...

As a company undergoing continual growth and transformation, CNOOD

所以，这些挑战不仅在我身上，更在每个CNOOD人身上，每天在发生。

CNOOD人共同创造了很多"Mission Impossible"，这一切都是我们发展的积淀，我们一直在创业的路上。

当下，公司第一次设立CEO岗，我有幸成为公司的第一任CEO，我深知任重道远，但我深信，有你们一如既往的关心、包容、信任、支持，并谨记老池的"跟随内心，止于至善"的八字赠言，我一定会兢兢业业，同大家一起从心出发，探索、续写CNOOD新篇章，实现我们共同的梦想！

provides us with many opportunities to grow with it.

Therefore, the challenges take place every day not only on me, but also on every CNOOD member.

Together, CNOOD members have carried out many a "Mission Impossible", which are the results of our development. We are forever on the way of entrepreneurship.

Now CNOOD sets the post of CEO for the first time, and I am lucky enough to be CNOOD's first CEO. I know the task is heavy and the way is long; nevertheless, with your usual caring love, forgiveness, trust and support, and Dennis' advice of "follow your heart, and achieve the supreme good", I firmly believe that I will work diligently, starting from the heart with all of you, to explore the new chapter of CNOOD's history and fulfill our common dreams!

李燕飞
Fay

毕业于上海对外经贸大学，脚踏实地，一步一个脚印走出每一个校园。
2006年，一句"未来，自己来创造"，开启国际贸易的职业之路。
2012年，进入CNOOD，做最真的自己，与伙伴们一起追梦，勇敢地去学习，去探索，去挑战。
生命是一次奇遇，曾以为已拥有很多，仰望星空，才发现真正的旅程才开启。

A graduate from Shanghai University of International Business and Economics, Fay has always been an earnest and down-to-earth person, walking with firm steps out of every campus.
She embarked on a career in the field of international trade in 2006, inspired by the words "I shall create the future myself".
She endeavors to be the truest self and seeks dreams with companions since she joined CNOOD in 2012, while learning, exploring and challenging bravely with them.
Life is an adventure. She used to think that she had already owned a lot, until she looks up at the stars and realizes that the true journey has just begun.

CNOOD 首任 CEO 就职典礼圆满举行
Inaugural Ceremony of CNOOD's First CEO Held with Great Success

■ Loreen

继往开来谱新章！

2017年3月1日，"CNOOD首任CEO李燕飞（Fay）就职典礼"在CNOOD上海环球大厦9楼办公室圆满举行。CNOOD上海办公室部分成员、CNOOD宁波结算中心一行、CNOOD香港分公司一行、江苏苏美达集团赵总一行、上海建工集团章总一行、中远海运特种运输股份有限公司杨总一行、中国出口信用保险公司黄总一行、德国莱茵大中华区张总一行以及部分海外客户参加了此次典礼。CNOOD南美分公司、西班牙分公司、海外部分合伙人虽不能亲临参加，但用贺电与花篮传达了他们最诚挚的祝贺。施璐德亚洲有限公司Charles（李鹏）主持仪式。

Carry on the Glorious Tradition and Open the Way to the Future

On March 1, 2017, the inaugural ceremony of Li Yanfei (Fay) as the first CEO of CNOOD was successfully held in the conference room on the 9th floor of CNOOD Shanghai. In addition to members of CNOOD Shanghai, CNOOD Ningbo Settlement Center and CNOOD Hong Kong Limited, among the guests attending the ceremony were: Mr. Zhao from SUMEC Group and his party, Mr. Zhang from Shanghai Construction Group and his party, Mr. Yang from COSCO Shipping Specialized Carriers Co., Ltd and his party, Mr. Huang from China Export & Credit Insurance Corporation (SINOSURE) and his party, Mr. Zhang form TUV Rheinland Greater China and his party, as well as part of our foreign clients. CNOOD Latam SPA from South America, CNOOD Engineering S.L. from Spain and some of its overseas partners, who were unable to attend the ceremony,

主持人主持典礼及介绍来宾

阳春三月，暖阳高照，万物峥嵘。在这个万象更新的大好季节，CNOOD 正朝着创立的第十个年头阔步前行。历时6个月，本着民主、透明、公正的原则，全体施璐德人投出了自己神圣而庄严的一票，我们郑重选出了自己的CEO。"互相关心，创造开心"是 CNOOD 发展的不竭动力与文化精髓所在。也借这次 CEO 就职仪式，在各位来宾的见证下，CNOOD 将跟随内心，从心出发，继续谱写 CNOOD 的新章。

also expressed their sincere congratulations through telegraph and flowers. Charles from CNOOD Asia Limited hosted the ceremony.

Host Conducting the Ceremony and the Guests

Bathed in the warm sun of March, all creatures were full of vitality. In this good, all-renewing season, CNOOD was striding towards the tenth year since its foundation. During these six months, guided by the principles of democracy, transparency and fairness, all CNOOD members had cast their holy and solemn votes, electing our own CEO. "Caring for each other and creating delightfulness" is the inexhaustible source of power for CNOOD's development and the very essence of its culture. With this inaugural ceremony, witnessed by all the

董事长池勇海致欢迎词并宣读任命书

池勇海先生（Dennis）首先代表施璐德亚洲有限公司全体员工欢迎各位来宾在百忙之中抽空而来，参与见证 CNOOD 具有里程碑意义的时刻。同时，饱含深情地对今天到场的来宾一一作了感谢。语言简单朴实，但情长而真切。Dennis "今天是一个感恩的日子，距我们办公室启动也已近 8 年。我们这 8 年的成长，离不开大家的支持。"

"感谢赵总，感谢苏美达！从 CNOOD 成立最初就一直伴随着我们，支持我们的成长。给予我们管理、业务、人才、资金等多方面的莫大支持！"

"感谢章总，感谢上海建工！带领我们走出了另外一条宽阔大道。是在章总的带领帮助下，凌晨 1 点仍然在项目一线的指导下，完成了 CNOOD 的第一个钢结构项目。我们还有很多的项目在路上……"

"感谢杨总，感谢中远海特！没有中远海特支持，就没有我们第一个钢结构项目顺利超预期的完成。我想未来的项目将以 DDP 和 DAP 为主导，这是趋势，这更是 CNOOD 的未来发展方向。我们所有的项目都是在朝着这个方向去走。"

attending guests, CNOOD would follow its inner calling and start from the heart, continuing to write a new chapter in its history.

Dennis' Welcoming Speech and the Appointment of CEO

At the beginning, Dennis welcomed the guests to witness the monumental moment for CNOOD on behalf of all the members of CNOOD Asia Limited. He expressed gratitude to every distinguished guest with deep feeling. The words were simple, but the emotion was genuine. "Today is a day of thanks, and it's nearly eight years since the opening of our office. Our growth in these eight years depends heavily on the support of everyone here." said Dennis.

He said, "Many thanks to Mr. Zhao and SUMEC! Thank you for being with us and supporting our growth since the foundation of CNOOD. Your supports to us in management, business, people, and funds are huge and substantial."

"Many thanks to Mr. Zhang and Shanghai Construction Group! Thank you for leading us onto a new broad way. It was with Mr. Zhang's direction and help, who worked until 1:00 a.m. at the site of project, that we were able to complete our first steel structure project. We have many more projects on the way …"

"Many thanks to Mr. Yang and COSCO Shipping Specialized Carriers! We could not have successfully completed our first steel structure project beyond expectation if not supported by COSCO Shipping Specialized Carriers. I believe that future projects will be mainly DDP and DAP. It is not only a trend

"我还要感谢TUV的张总,是TUV的支持让我们走到今天。我们在早期是没有自己专业的质控部门的,TUV就是我们的质量管理。我要感谢黄总,感谢中信保。让我们更加大胆地做项目,做投资,给客户提供满意的服务。做到零索赔,项目质量我们自己把控,而风险我们则交给中信保。"

"今天,我们只是邀请了很少的一部分人,但是需要感谢的人很多。我们会用我们的业务感谢支持我们的伙伴,用我们的服务感谢我们的客户。巾短情长,我们把感恩的心放在心里。"

but also the direction of future development for CNOOD, toward which all our projects are being directed."

He said, "I would also like to thank Mr. Zhang of TUV. It is TUV that has supported us all the way here. In the early days, we did not have our own quality control department, and TUV *was* our quality control. I would like to thank Mr. Huang and SINOSURE for allowing us to carry out projects and make investments more boldly, and provide satisfying services to clients. To achieve the goal of zero-claim, we control the quality of projects, and SINOSURE will take care of risks."

"Today we only invite a small number of guests, but our gratitude is due to a lot more people. We will express our gratitude to companions who support us with business, and our gratitude to the clients with our services. Time is limited, while my feelings are deep. We will cherish the gratitude in our heart." Dennis said.

随后，Dennis宣读了李燕飞女士就任施璐德首任CEO的任命文件，并为李燕飞女士颁发任命书。

李燕飞发表就职演讲

李燕飞女士给大家分享回顾了自己十一年工作历程，带团队十年来自己的成长与体会。回首了自己加入CNOOD，并成为合伙人这些年来所见、所闻、所感、所悟。

"在CNOOD如何带领好一个团队？只要真心对成员们好，用心陪伴他们成长就好。为什么CNOOD能让人一直想成长、在成长？因为这里不仅有许多杰出的人，更重要的是大家都愿意培养人，帮助人，关心人。上善若水，厚德载物。

After that, Dennis announced the appointment of Li Yanfei (Fay) as the first CEO of CNOOD, and presented her with the appointment letter.

Inaugural Speech by Fay

Fay shared with everyone her growth and experience during the eleven years of working and the ten years as a team-leader. She recalled what she saw, heard, felt and understood since she joined CNOOD and became a partner.

"How to lead a team successfully in CNOOD? If you're truly doing things to their benefit, and be with them whole-heartedly when they grow up, that's enough. Why could CNOOD make people want to grow and keep growing all the time? It's not only because we have a galaxy of talent but also because everyone here is willing to nurture, help and care for others. The supreme

在施璐德我有什么事情是该不该做的或者是能不能做的？在这里，只要你敢想，想做，CNOOD 就是你坚强的后盾。组织第一次校园宣讲会、组织第一次公司春游、签订第一份与第三方检验公司的长协、编制第一份业务操作手册与公司宣传册、不停打破出差时间极限以让 CNOOD 走向更多的市场与领域、在施璐德一直在做最好最真的自己，一直在突破自己的路上……

我来到施璐德这些年，见证并且参与了施璐德的所有变化：合伙人团队更加完善，全球分公司和市场布局越来越全面，质量管理体系建立得越来越健全，商业模式不断升级转型，公司内各部门搭建越来越合理……

这些成长，不仅在我身上，更在每个 CNOOD 人身上，每天在发生。CNOOD 人共同创造了很多 'Mission Impossible'，这一切都是我们发展的积淀，我们一直在创业的路上。"

（更多内容，请参阅李燕飞女士就职发言全文。）

goodwill resembles the nature of water; a person with great virtue can take on greater responsibilities.

In CNOOD, is there anything that we would ask ourselves:"Should I do it or not?" or "Can I do it or not?" You will be strongly backed by CNOOD if you have the courage of imagination and the desire of achieving something. Organizing CNOOD's first campus recruitment activity and its first spring outing; signing CNOOD's first long-term agreement with a TPI firm; preparing CNOOD's first Work-manual for business operation; breaking repeatedly the records of the time on business trip to take CNOOD to more markets and areas: I have always tried to be the best, truest self. I am forever on the way of self-breakthrough …

During the years since I came to CNOOD, I have witnessed and participated in all its changes: the team of partners has been improved; the global distribution of branch companies and markets are becoming more and more comprehensive; quality control system is being perfected; the business model is going through upgrading and transformation; the structure of departments within the company are being rationalized.

The growth takes place every day not only on me, but also on every CNOOD member. Together, CNOOD members have carried out many a 'Mission Impossible', which are the results of our development. We are forever on the way of entrepreneurship."

(For more information, please refer to the whole text of the inaugural speech made by Fay.)

合作伙伴发言助力送祝福

苏美达赵总首先表达了他的感谢之情，感谢能来见证 CNOOD 具有里程碑意义的重要时刻。赵总表示与 CNOOD 合作这么多年，感受到了 CNOOD 很多值得学习的地方。赵总总结为：（1）CNOOD 是一个具有强烈发展欲望和创新精神的创业团队；（2）CNOOD 选择的道路是符合时代潮流的、符合"一带一路"、符合中国产业转型升级的，有时候方向比努力更重要；（3）CNOOD 人都非常向上，具有正气和正能量，有着一股向上的力量；（4）CNOOD 非常透明和开放，民主开放，内外一样与客户合作的沟通非常充分。最后赵总表示，苏美达也一直在致力成为现代服务业的先行者，民营企业的助力者。CNOOD 选择了苏美达，也是给了他们使

Mr. Zhao from SUMEC Group first expressed his gratitude for being invited to witness this monumental moment of CNOOD. He told everyone that he had discovered, during so many years of cooperation, many features in CNOOD that worth learning, which he summed up as follows: (1) CNOOD is an entrepreneurial team with a strong desire to develop and the spirit of innovation. (2) The way CNOOD has chosen is in keeping with the trends of our times, the Belt and Road Initiative, and the transformation and upgrading of China's domestic industries. Sometimes the direction is more important than the effort itself. (3) All CNOOD members have

命，希望在以后的合作中，大家一起进步，一起成长。

上海建工集团章总和大家分享了与CNOOD正式合作一年来的体会。虽然合作时间并不是特别长，但是CNOOD这个企业的文化、价值观、理念、作风给他和上海建工带来了不一样的感受。他说道，"CNOOD是一家具有现代化企业理念的公司，是中国新兴企业的发展代表。在很多企业以利当先时，CNOOD揽天下英才为其所用，大家民主，似家人，用情怀做事。相信施璐德这个'火炬'将燃遍全球。上海建工也将做好坚强的后盾，特别是在钢结构这块为施璐德助力！"

中远海特的杨总则先代表中远海运特种运输股份有限公司祝贺CNOOD选出了德才兼备、蕙心兰质的CEO。然后他表示，作为CNOOD的合作伙伴，中远海

high morale with integrity and positive energy, having a power to move forward. (4) CNOOD is very transparent and open, communicating thoroughly in its cooperation with others, and demonstrating democracy and open-mindedness to both internal and external parties. He concluded that SUMEC had been doing its best to be a pioneer in modern services and a booster for private-sector enterprises. When CNOOD chose SUMEC, it also gave us a mission. I hope both companies will make progress and grow up together in further cooperation.

Mr. Zhang from Shanghai Construction Group shared with everyone his experience during one year's cooperation with CNOOD. Though the time was not very long, he and Shanghai Construction Group were both impressed by the different culture, values, ideas of CNOOD and its way of treating others. He said, "CNOOD is a company with modern ideas, and a developing representative of the emerging enterprises. While many companies focus primarily on profits, CNOOD gathers around it talented people all over the world to serve a common purpose. All its members make decisions in a democratic manner like a family, and doing things with feelings. I believe that the 'torch' of CNOOD will send flames to the whole world. Shanghai Construction Group will give strong backing to CNOOD, especially helping it in the field of steel structure!"

Mr. Yang, on behalf of COSCO Shipping Specialized Carriers Co., Ltd, congratulated CNOOD for having elected a CEO with ability and integrity, pure heart and fine

特见证并参与支持了CNOOD第一个钢结构项目的顺利完成。CNOOD自运营八年以来,取得了一系列的成绩,在国际多处设立了办事处与分公司,遍及非洲、中东、南美、澳洲等。以其独特的经营理念、平台化、专业化、项目团队制等优势,CNOOD诚信经营,迅速发展,赢得了市场与客户的信赖。中远海特的目标是成为大型工程项目设备运输的引导者。在当下航运界的困境,中远海特主动求新求变,摒弃传统船东思维,不断推进自己的结构提升与服务升级,已逐步实现从传统船东向服务型船东转型。"在此,我代表中远海特向我们的合作伙伴郑重承诺:我们将全力以赴,以举重若轻的合力,举轻若重的精神执行好CNOOD的每一个项目,为贵司业务发展提供更好的保障,在迈向中远海特战略目标征程上,我们将与CNOOD携手同行,真诚合作,共同发展!"杨总郑重的承诺,也将大家喜悦与激动的心情点燃到了极致!

quality. He then said that COSCO Shipping Specialized Carriers, as a cooperative partner of CNOOD, had witnessed and participated in supporting the successful completion of CNOOD's first steel structure project. CNOOD had made a series of achievements, establishing offices and branch companies in various countries with projects in Africa, Middle East, South America and Australia etc. It grew rapidly and won the trust of market and clients by doing business honestly with its unique business ideas such as platform-based operation, specialization and project team etc. In the meantime, COSCO Shipping Specialized Carriers aimed to be the leader in the field of large-scale engineering project equipment transport. Facing the difficult situation in the shipping industry, it took the initiative to seek innovation and changes, casting away the old-fashioned way of thinking as a ship-owner. It had been continuously pushing the process of upgrading its structure and service, gradually transforming from a traditional ship-owner into a service-oriented one. "At this moment, I solemnly promise to our cooperative partner, on behalf of COSCO Shipping Specialized Carriers: We shall do our best to carry out every project of CNOOD with the great capability and the meticulous spirit, providing better guarantee to your business development. In the journey toward our strategic goal, we shall go hand in hand with CNOOD, sincerely working together with you for common development!" The solemn promise made by Mr. Yang brought the joyful and exciting atmosphere to the climax.

江苏苏美达集团赵总
Mr. Zhao from SUMEC Group

上海建工集团章总
Mr. Zhang from Shanghai Construction Group

中远海运特种运输股份有限公司杨总
Mr. Yang from COSCO Shipping Specialized Carriers Co., Ltd

特别纪念：感恩 & 传承

这次我们为首任 CEO 就职典礼还专门定制了纪念币。纪念币正面是公司的名称与 Logo，背面一幅以手浇灌小树苗的图案，载有"感恩有您，从心出发"：CNOOD 感恩所有对 CNOOD 成长的关心与帮助，感恩社会的抚育；CNOOD 对每一位 CNOOD 人的呵护与培养，CNOOD 的伙伴对 CNOOD 成长的帮助与成就，CNOOD 人与 CNOOD 伙伴对新任 CEO 以及管理团队的信任与展望；小树苗的破土而出，茁壮成长，它的生机与活力也象征着 CNOOD 人与 CNOOD 正带着无限的希望与热情走在全新的里程上。

Special Memory: Gratitude & Inheritance

We prepared a special set of made-to-order commemorative coins for the inaugural ceremony of the first CEO of CNOOD. On the obverse of the coin was the company's name and logo; on the reverse was a design of a sapling being watered by a hand, with the words "gratitude to you; start from the heart". It stood for CNOOD's gratitude to all who cared for and helped with its growth, and the gratitude to the fostering of the society; it also stood for CNOOD's protection and nurturing to every CNOOD member, the help in achieving CNOOD's growth offered by its cooperative partners, as well as the trust and prospect by all CNOOD members and companions to the new CEO and the managerial team. The vitality and vigor of the sapling, which was breaking through the

soil and growing up sturdily, represented all CNOOD members and the company on the brand-new journey with boundless hope and enthusiasm.

下午茶趴

典礼仪式结束后，就是大家自由交谈的下午茶 Party 啦！纪念大蛋糕、精致点心、美酒水果，聊天拍照，情谊绵长！

Afternoon Tea Party

After the ceremony was the time for afternoon tea party, when we conversed freely with cake for commemoration, delicate desserts, wine and fruits. We chatted warmly and took photos. What deep friendly feelings!

未完待续，我们一直在路上……

This is NOT THE END. We are ever on the way ...

罗蓉
Loreen

Loreen，2014年硕士毕业于东华大学，随后正式加入施璐德。性格活泼开朗，但也冷静沉着。最害怕被"大众"同化，希望永葆独立的精神和不怕做奇葩的事情。

Loreen formally joined CNOOD soon after graduating from Donghua University with a master's degree in 2014. With a lively and cheerful disposition, she is also calm and cool-headed. What she fears most is being assimilated by "the masses". She hopes to maintain the spirit of independence forever, never afraid of doing "weird" things.

行　走

Walking

■ Jeff Xu

生活，最重要的是开心。

工作，是生活的一部分，而且是很大的一部分。

所以，我们才更要做自己喜欢的工作。

只有发自内心的热爱，才会全情投入，才会乐此不疲。

我很幸运，毕业之际能与施璐德美丽邂逅，做着自己热爱的工作，过着自己中意的生活。

"相互关心，创造开心；相互关怀，共同成长；跟随内心，勇往直前。"

在施璐德大家庭一年了，对这二十四个字我有着切身且深刻的体会。

一年多姿多彩的工作中，有太多太多的欢笑与喜悦。

虽也曾纠结过、彷徨过、沮丧过、胆怯过，却从来没有退缩过。

Delightfulness is what matters most in life.

Work is a part—and a very big part—of life.

Therefore, we are in a greater need for work that we enjoy.

Only deep love from the bottom of heart engenders commitment with all your soul, never feeling fatigued.

It is lucky for me to have met CNOOD by an excellent chance, doing the work I love and living the life to my liking.

"Care for each other and create delightfulness; take care of each other and grow together; follow the heart and advance bravely." I now get a personal and deep understanding of these words after being in the big family of CNOOD for one year.

The one year of work in CNOOD has been colored with too much laughter and joy.

Although once perplexed, confused, frustrated and intimidated, I have never flinched.

有施璐德大家庭的关心与支持，让我更加勇敢面对挫折与困难。

人生是一场修行，听从自己内心的声音，走好生命中的每一步！

With the caring support from the big family of CNOOD, I am able to face all the setbacks and hardships more bravely.

Be a better man!
Life is a spiritual practice. Hearken to the voice in your heart, and take firmly every step in life!
Be a better man!

徐志锋
Jeff Xu

2016年3月毕业于上海大学，通过校园招聘与施璐德结缘并有幸成为施璐德大家庭的一分子。在施璐德一年的时间里，跟随自己的内心，从心出发，快乐学习，快乐成长，勇敢面对生活和工作中的种种挑战，勇往直前，努力做最好的自己！

Graduating from Shanghai University in March 2016, Jeff Xu became a member of the big family of CNOOD via campus recruitment. Following and starting from the heart, he has been learning and working happily during the one year in CNOOD. Facing the challenges in both the life and work, he is doing his best and marching forward courageously!

新芽在这里成长，梦想从这里起航
Here is the Place Where New Buds Grow, and Dreams Start

■ Jenna

还记得 Dennis 在 2015 年春节后的一次分享——新芽，遥不可及的梦想。初出校园，第一份工作便是在 CNOOD，初入职场的我就像是一株新芽，在 CNOOD 这片沃土中生长。最近各大 app 都流行用"足迹"来总结过去的一年，以下就是我加入 CNOOD 后一年多的"足迹"。

常熟

常熟是我在 CNOOD 的第一站，有幸见证了常熟加工中心，即如今的施璐德装备制造（常熟）有限公司的诞生。第一次到常熟，天气还比较冷，港口的风大，六号库空荡荡的，地也不平。后来，地整平了，内外焊机、滚轮架到了，防腐线建起来了。到后来的第一根管子出库，第一个项目结束，我深深为我们 CNOOD 感到自豪。通过这个项目，我有了更深刻的体会，那就是 CNOOD 愿意给大家一个广阔的平

I still remember what Dennis shared with us shortly after the Spring Festival of 2015—"New Bud, and the unapproachable Dream". Just graduating from college, I worked at CNOOD as my first job. A freshman in the company, I was just like a new bud growing in the fertile soil of CNOOD. Recently, it is popular with apps to summarize the last year by "footprints". The following are my "footprints" during the time more than one year since I joined CNOOD.

Changshu

Changshu was my first stop in CNOOD, where I was lucky enough to witness the birth of Changshu Processing Center, which later became CNOOD Equipment Manufacturing (Changshu) Co., Ltd. It was still cold when we arrived in Changshu for the first time, with strong winds around the port. The No. Six Warehouse was all empty; the ground was uneven, too. Later, the ground was leveled, internal and external welders arrived, and the

台，放手让大家去做。在这样的环境中，一个人才会发挥自己的主观能动性，激发出自己的潜能。任何事情，只要下定决心，用心去做，努力付出，就都能做到。在这里，我见识到了CNOOD的魄力和努力。

沙市

沙市是我正式入职后的第一站，在这里系统地执行了一个项目。从前期技术文件的确认，到项目推进，及项目中问题的协调解决，我知道了如何与工厂沟通。这个项目是CNOOD与沙市钢管厂的第一次合作。项目初期，我们有过磨合，随着项目的进行，大家的合作越来越顺畅，我们的工作模式得到了高度认可和赞赏。在这里，我见识到了CNOOD的魅力。

天津

天津TPCO的项目是我独立执行的第一个项目，让我对一直比较陌生的物流、报关等环节有了更深的理解。在这个项目中，我第一次在项目中跟客户直接沟通，使我在采购环节站在销售立场执行一个项目。独立执行项目需要综合考虑、统

corrosion protection line was built. When the first pipe was delivered from the stock and when the first project was completed, I was deeply proud of CNOOD. With this project, I get a deep understanding that CNOOD is willing to offer everyone a broad platform, where all of us can work freely. Only in such an atmosphere can one bring initiative into full play and activate one's potentiality. We can do anything if we are determined and do our best wholeheartedly. Here, I saw the guts and endeavor of CNOOD.

Shashi

Shashi was my first stop since I formally join CNOOD, where I carried out a project from the very beginning. From confirmation of technical documentation to project progress, and problem solving in the process of the project, I learned the way of communicating with factories. This project was the first cooperation between CNOOD and Shashi Steel Pipe Factory. We experienced running-in during the initial stage. As the project proceeded, the cooperation between us got smoother and smoother, and our way of working was highly recognized and appreciated. Here, I saw the charm of CNOOD.

Tianjin

The TPCO project in Tianjin was the first one I carried out independently, allowing me to get a deeper understanding of logistics, customs declaration etc., with which I was previously somewhat unfamiliar. In this project, I was involved in direct

筹安排许多环节，得到的收获和满足感也是最大的。夕阳西下，当我拍下最后一个集装箱的铅封的一刻，我体会到了作为一名 CNOOD 人的责任感。

海门

在上海建工（江苏）钢结构有限公司，我执行了第一个钢结构项目，这对于我是一个全新的领域。随着项目的进行，前几批货物的发出，我们得到了更多的项目，这是客户对我们的认可和信任。这个项目历时四个多月，是我执行过的项目中时间最长的，它让我对项目执行有了更深的体会。机会总是给有准备的人，脚踏实地才能更好地仰望星空，只要用心付出，一定能得到好的回报。通过这个项目，我看到了 CNOOD 的明天。

以上就是我加入 CNOOD 后几个主要的"脚印"，串起了我一年多来的"足迹"。虽然我加入 CNOOD 的时间不久，但深深感受到了 CNOOD 的魅力，尤其是出差很久后回到办公室，会有一种归属感，让人平静。CNOOD 就像一个温暖的大家庭，

communication with a client. This enabled me to conduct a project from both the purchasing and sales points of view. When I carried out a project independently, I need to take many factors into account and make overall plans accordingly. I gained the most from the process, and my satisfaction was also the greatest. The moment I took a photo of the seal of the last container, as the sun was setting in the west, I felt the sense of duty as a CNOOD member.

Haimen

With Shanghai Construction (Jiangsu) Steel Structure Co., Ltd., I carried out my first steel structure project, which was an entirely new to me. With the progress of project, the first couple batches of products were delivered, and we got more projects because of the client's recognition of and trust on us. This project lasted for over four months, which cost the longest time in all the projects I had carried out. It enabled me to have a deeper understanding of project management. Opportunities are only for prepared minds; you can look up at stars only if you plant your feet firmly on the ground. You will be amply rewarded so long as you make commitment wholeheartedly. Through this project, I saw the future of CNOOD.

Above are some of my major "footprints" since I joined CNOOD. Though I joined CNOOD not very long ago, I have deeply felt the charm of it, especially the sense of belonging that makes me calm down when I return to the office after a long business trip.

大家庭里的人们相互关心；这个大家庭也需要我们每个人的守护，使之绽放更多的绚烂，创造更多的开心。

CNOOD is a big, warm family, with members caring for each other. Meanwhile, the big family itself needs the guard from everyone, rendering it more splendid and creating more delightfulness.

胡静航
Jenna

2015 年 6 月毕业于复旦大学材料科学系，2015 年 7 月正式加入 CNOOD，是人生中第一份工作。脚踏实地、仰望星空是之前学习和现在工作中的座右铭。

Jenna graduated from the Department of Materials Science, Fudan University in June 2015 and joined CNOOD in July of the same year as the first job in her lifetime. "Plant your feet firmly on the ground and look up at the stars" is her motto both in college and in workplace.

质量卓越 | 价格最优 | 服务真诚 | 持续改进
Supreme Quality | Superior Price | Sincere Service | Sustaining Improvement

■ Lay

质量，守护着公司，保卫着行业。

从公司创立之初，CNOOD 就以全过程质量管理为基础，秉持提供满足并超越客户期望的高品质产品和服务的理念，打造了 CNOOD 品牌的精品形象。

转眼已经马上就要进入 2017 年，在过去的一年，对于 CNOOD 来说是不凡的一年。质量部发生了多项变化，在公司发展过程中发挥了重要作用。

2016 的质量部：
1. 新的专业合伙人

契合公司发展和转型需求，2016 年质量部新增了钢结构和项目管理领域方面的专业合伙人。为公司在钢构领域的市场提供了支持和现场管理，增加了竞争力和公司整体的技术实力。

Quality—it safeguards the company as well as the whole industry.

Ever since its foundation, CNOOD has created an exceptional brand image on the basis of whole-process quality control, by providing high-quality products and services that not only satisfy but also surpass customer expectations.

We will soon usher in the year 2017, while 2016 has been an extraordinary year for CNOOD. The QC Department saw a number of changes, and played an important role in the growth of the company.

The QC Department in 2016:

1. New professional partner

Fitting in with the company's development and transformation, professional partner in the fields of steel structure and project management newly joined the QC Department in 2016, which will provide support and on-site management for the company in the steel structure market and hence enhance the competitive advantage and technological

2. 新的 TPI 公司

在新的市场领域内，公司引入了新的专业 TPI 公司：

NOV Tuboscope，全球最大的石油天然气钻探设备供应商国民油井（NOV）的第三方检验公司，主要负责钢结构产品的全过程第三方监造。2016 年参与了公司 IMI 项目的监造。

DNVGL，挪威船级社（DNV）与德国劳氏船级社（GL）合并的集团公司。目前公司已经与其工业部签署了战略合作协议，主要负责海工产品的全过程第三方监造。2016 年参与了公司 IMI 项目中气囊产品的监造。

competence of the company as a whole.

2. New TPI firms

The company introduced new professional TPI firms in new markets:

—NOV Tuboscope, a TPI company of NOV, the world's largest supplier of oil & gas drilling equipments, engaged primarily for whole-process third party supervision of steel structure products. In 2016, it participated in the supervision of CNOOD's IMI project.

—DNVGL, a group company by merging Det Norske Veritas (DNV) and Germanischer Lloyd (GL). CNOOD has signed an agreement for strategic cooperation with its Industry Department. It is engaged chiefly for whole-process third party supervision

深圳金盛工程设备有限公司（SZJS），专业的测量公司，主要采用光学仪器进行空间测量，并能提供质量上乘的测量结果和报告，为IMI项目导管架的制作提供了支持。

振华检测，是振华重工集团下属的检测公司，在国内有三家CNAS认证实验室，其能力覆盖了钢结构产品制作全过程中各类实验和检测要求，且极具价格优势。

3. 新的钢结构项目管理

钢结构施工在整个项目施工中的关键路径上，其管理在整个项目中的位置非常重要，管理水平高低也直接影响整个项目运行好坏。通过对设计资源、物料资源、生产资源、检验资源和物流资源的有效整合，CNOOD为业主的整个项目提升了近30%的进度预期，第一批6只导管架13天的制作周期堪称奇迹。赢得了客户的美誉和信任。

4. 新的管理系统

PI系统（Performance & Improvement System）是CNOOD的质量环境和职业健

of marine engineering products. In 2016, it participated in the supervision of gasbag products in CNOOD's IMI project.

—Shenzhen Jinsheng Engineering Equipment Co., Ltd. (SZJS), a professional surveying company who specializes in spatial measurement using optical instruments, providing high-quality survey results and reports. It has supported the manufacture of jackets in the IMI project.

—ZPMC Inspection, an inspection company subsidiary to Shanghai Zhenhua Heavy Industry Co., Ltd. (ZPMC) who owned three CNAS accredited laboratories in China, covering various experiment and inspection requirements in the whole process of steel structure products manufacture, with an exceptional advantage in price.

3. New steel structure project management

The management of steel structure construction, which is on the key path of construction of the project, is of critical importance to the project and has a direct impact on the operational results of it. Through effective integration of the resources of design, materials, production, inspection and logistics, CNOOD has successfully accelerated the expected rate of progress by nearly 30% for the owner of the project. It could almost be called a miracle that the construction of the first six jackets was completed in merely 13 days. The accomplishment has helped CNOOD to obtain reputation among and trust from clients.

4. New management system

The Performance & Improvement (PI) System is short for the CNOOD version of

康安全体系的简称。其体系文件策划半年并于 2016 年 11 月 15 日正式发布。目前共发布了 124 份受控文件，文本量近 20 万字。随着体系文件的设立，后续的支援系统正在开发并完善，将大大增强公司的核心实力。

5. 新的工厂认证

2016 年，常熟工厂先后通过了：欧标钢结构和铝结构施工资质 EXC3 级（EN1090 EXC 3），欧标金属材料熔化焊焊接质量认证（ISO 3834），欧标热轧钢管制造认证（EN10210），欧标冷成型结构钢管制造认证（EN10219），质量管理体系认证（ISO 9001）。

2016 年从心出发，坚守本心，CNOOD 成长的脚步从未停止。

2017 年重新出发，质量部继续为公司的蓬勃发展，保驾护航。

Quality, Environment, Occupational Health and Safety Management System. The planning of the system documents took half a year, and the system was officially announced on November 15, 2016. Up to now, 124 controlled documents have been issued, containing nearly 200 thousand words. With the establishment of the system documents, follow-up supporting systems are being developed and improved, which will greatly strengthen CNOOD's core competence.

5. New manufacture certification

In 2016, CNOOD Changshu Processing Center fulfilled the following certifications: European quality standard for all steel and aluminum structures EXC Level 3 (EN1090 EXC3), European quality certification for fusion welding of metallic materials (ISO 3834), European certification for hot finished steel tube manufacture (EN10210), European certification for cold formed structural steel tube (EN10219), and quality management systems certification (ISO 9001).

During the year 2016, starting from the heart and sticking to initial aspiration, CNOOD never stopped its pace of growing.

In the year 2017, departing from a new start, the QC Department will continue safeguarding the vigorous growth of CNOOD.

陶磊
Lay

1986年2月出生上海,毕业于上海工程技术大学,曾在大型跨国国企以及知名外资公司任关键职位,对项目管理和质量控制有丰富经验。

Tao Lei (Lay) was born in Shanghai in February 1986. Graduating from Shanghai University of Engineering Science, he held key positions in large transnational state-owned enterprises and famous foreign companies, with rich experience in project management and quality control.

一个无边际的系统
A System without Boundary

■ Nick

最早提出这个系统的概念，还是在2014年年底，我同老池、振震一起，边吃边谈。那时候的概念还很泛很模糊，但是大家都很兴奋，为我们谈论的一个崭新的无边际的系统。我们期望创建一个系统，它适用于绝大部分的场景，可以让任何人加入进来，工作、学习、成长、分享等等。我们要集合大家的智慧，同时让这些智慧服务于大家。

之后到2015年5月，振震和我正式加入CNOOD，甩开膀子开始了研发。最初的系统研发并不顺利，需求沟通不够透彻，许多功能多次推翻重做，最后终于在2015年9月22日，我们发布了正式版本，也是我们研发的第5个版本。发布的时候，很激动也很忐忑。我们构想的系统，经过不断打磨，终于面世了。然而它还有很多欠缺，很多不完善，不知道它是否经受得起考验。不管怎样，它开始提供服务了，我们会让它一直服务下去。

It was at the end of 2014 that the idea of "system" was proposed, when Dennis, Ken and I were having dinner and talking together. Though it was still general, vague in nature at that time, everyone was excited for the brand-new system without border that we were talking about. We expected to create a system that is applicable to most scenarios and allows anyone to join in working, studying, growing, sharing, etc. We aimed to pool the wisdom of everyone, while making this wisdom serve everyone.

Later on, Zhenzhen and I formally joined CNOOD in May, 2015, and began to go all out in the R & D of the system. However, the process was not quite smooth initially. Many functions had to be re-developed several times due to insufficient communication about users' demands. On September 22, 2015, we finally released the official version—and also the fifth version we had developed—of the system. We felt excited and uneasy at the same time.

接下来的一年多时间，整个系统快速迭代开发，实现了一个巨大的提升。我们广泛收集系统用户的反馈，同时不断加深自身对系统的理解，让系统提供更优质的服务。整个系统包含许许多多的小系统，其中的核心是 Workbench。基于这个核心，不同的小系统提供不同的功能，以此构建整个完整的系统。我们先后发布了 Finance 系统、官网、微信服务号、身份验证系统、BBS 系统、Decison 系统、API 系统、Open 系统、PI 系统、User Center 系统、CRM 系统等。在 2016 年，很重要的一个里程碑是我们对外开放了部分功能，让整个系统不是单单地服务于 CNOOD，而是更多的人。未来，我们还将更全面地开放。下图为系统的一个基本框架。有的已经实现，但还需不断优化；有的正在开发当中，即将面世；还有的尚在开发计划中。

On one hand, the system we conceived eventually came out after numerous refinements. On the other, it still had a number of deficiencies and imperfections, and we were not sure whether or not it could stand the test. In any case, as long as it began to provide service, we should make it go on infinitely.

During the following days more than a year, the whole system has been enhanced profoundly through fast iterative development. We have exhaustively gathered user feedbacks, while in the meantime continuously deepening our understanding of the system, ensuring to deliver services of higher quality. The system as a whole comprises numerous sub-systems, the core of which is Workbench. Based on it, various functions are available via different sub-systems, thus constructing a complete system. We have launched, one after another, the Finance System, Official Website, WeChat Official Account, Identity Verification System, BBS System, Decision System, API System, Open System, PI System, User Center System, CRM System, etc. A critical milestone in the year 2016 was that we opened a part of the functions to the public, so that the system served more people instead of serving only CNOOD. We are planning a more thorough opening in the future. The figure below shows the underlying framework of the system. Some have been actualized and need continuous optimization, and some are in the R&D stage and will soon come out, while others are only in the planning for further R&D.

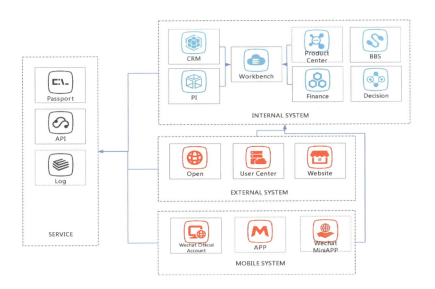

新的一年,我们还有很多事情要做,系统也有很多功能要去实现。我们要新增和优化很多功能,也要加强移动端的研发。现在它还很小,提供的服务也有限。不过我们相信,只要坚持和努力,我们会向着无边际系统的目标不断靠近。

We still get a lot of things to do in the year 2017; as for the system, there are yet many functions to actualize. We will add a number of new functions and optimize the existing ones, while furthering the mobile-end R&D. Currently it's still very small and the services it provides are limited. However, we believe that we will be nearer and nearer to the goal of a system without boundary.

注：徐振震，Nick 好搭档，施璐德 DT 部门合伙人。
Note: Ken, the best partner of Nick in CNOOD DT department.

张牛 / Nick

张牛，东华大学计算机硕士研究生。毕业后加入腾讯公司，于 2015 年加入 CNOOD。深耕系统研发，产品设计。兴趣爱好广泛，非典型程序员一名。

Nick joined Tencent after graduating from Donghua University with a master's degree in Computer Science. Later, he joined CNOOD in 2015. He devotes himself to system R&D and product design. With a wide range of interests, he considers himself as an atypical programmer.

从开端到另一个开端
From One Beginning to Another

■ Billy

1. 从开端到另一个开端

这个标题也许是我在经过在施璐德这么多年下来的直接感悟。

6年多的时光一晃而过,公司实现从一般贸易到工程贸易再到工程公司雏形的转变,点点滴滴,历历在目。

在过程中,有无数的供应商和行业同行见证了我们从一个起点到另一个起点,总认为我们将无法继续下去,但一个一个奇迹总在最艰难的时候出现,坚持我们的信念成为奇迹的来源。

2. 从分享得到收获

2016年,我也有幸参与了2016年新人培训的组织工作,从制订培训计划和参与培训分享,到安排工厂参观。

1. From One Beginning to Another

This title might be an expression of my first-hand perception after the years I have been with CNOOD.

The time of more than six years quickly passed even before we are aware of it. CNOOD has transformed from general trade to engineering trade, and again to the embryonic form of an engineering firm. I can still vividly picture every bit of the transformation in my mind's eye.

During this process, numerous suppliers and fellow traders have witnessed our progress from one beginning to another. Every time, they did not think we could move on. However, miracles appeared, one after another, always at the most difficult moment. Our persistent conviction has been the source of the miracles.

2. Rewards of Sharing

In 2016, I also had the honor to take part in organizing the orientation program for new staff members, from program planning

其实在这个系列的工作中，我无疑是收获很大的，这让我对于公司文化、工作方式、产品了解、业务模式都系统性地巩固了一遍。

也从新同事的问题中得到自己所没有考虑到或者总结到的新知识，这也是从公司一开始我们不停地分享中得到更多的收获。

同时，在2016年有幸与新同事Jeff共事，Jeff的学习能力很强，工作也上心，在我们共同做项目的时候，我分享了我对于生产中的控制点，但从Jeff的反馈中体会到不断倒空自己的过程中才能学到新的知识，不然会被所谓的经验冲淡自己更深入学习的热情。

and sharing, to the arrangement of factory visiting.

Without doubt, I gained a lot from these assignments, which allowed me to get more familiar with the corporate culture, working approaches, product knowledge and business model of the company.

From the questions raised by new colleagues, I also obtained new knowledge that I have never considered nor summed up, in the way that we have gained more from continuous sharing ever since the fountain of CNOOD.

In the meantime, I was also lucky to work with my new colleague Jeff, who had strong learning ability and paid great attention to his work. When we worked together on a project, I shared my opinion about control points in the production. But Jeff's feedback made me realize that one can learn new things only

也期盼在新的一年里和 Jeff 有更多的合作和分享，一起提高自己的能力，一起学习新的产品，一起跟进市场的需求。

3. 制订工作的方向

2016 年，很多资深的合伙人加入我们的公司，特别有幸，Paul Chen 作为我的导师也同时作为我们工作组的领导，带我们接触了真正行业的用户、业主、工程公司、行业内的优秀供应商和制造商。

这使我们公司真正发展到工程公司迈出了历史性的一步。

by ceaselessly emptying oneself, otherwise his enthusiasm for further learning would be diluted by so called "experience".

I wish I could have more opportunities to work together and share with Jeff. Together shall we enhance our capabilities, learn about new products, and follow the demands on the market.

3. Setting the Direction of Work

In 2016, many senior partners joined our company. Especially, it was lucky for me that Paul Chen, my tutor and the leader of our work group, introduced us to customers, owners, engineering firms, as well as outstanding suppliers and manufacturers in the industry.

This is a step of historic significance in our way towards a true engineering firm.

这也使我对于现两年的工作方向有了明确的导向。

（1）对于市场：我们要真正了解业主与工程公司的需求，要在他们的产业链条上带来价值增加的服务；

（2）对于产品：我们的产品导向将从单一产品到模块化生产的转变；

（3）对于我们自己：我们自己的能力提升太关键，我们要尽快学习项目管理的知识并落实于工作中。

This also allows me to be clearly oriented about the direction of my work in the coming few years.

(1) As to the market: We should truly understand the demands of owners and engineering firms, and provide value-adding services in their industry chains.

(2) As to the products: Our products will shift from single-product mode to modular production.

(3) As to ourselves: It is critical to promote our own capabilities, and we shall learn, as soon as possible, the knowledge of project management and put it into work.

顾天阳
Billy

顾天阳，2010年正式加入施璐德，工作至今，现为公司经理，MBA学历。见证了施璐德每一个起点，每一个奇迹的发生。从一般贸易到工程贸易，从工程贸易到项目采购中心，现在又在为公司成为真正的EPC工程公司而努力。相信：一切不是最好就没到最后。

Billy has been working at CNOOD ASIA LIMITED since he formally joined the company in 2010. Now he is a manager in CNOOD with an MBA degree. He has witnessed every starting point of CNOOD and every time a miracle occurred. Having seen the transformation of CNOOD as a company focused on general trade to one engaged in engineering trade, and again to a project procurement center, now he is making efforts to help CNOOD become a true EPC company. He believes that it is not the end if everything is not the best.

在施璐德工作的体会
WORKING AT CNOOD

■ Nicolas Kipreos

少点索取，多些奉献；
更多机遇，与你相伴。
携手客户，克服万难；
施璐德人，矢志领先。

Expect less and give us more
Increased opportunities therefore
Yes, overcoming whatever challenges may face customers,
We'll exceed. We are Cnood members.

少点索取，多些奉献；
夙兴夜寐，勇于登攀。
倾注全力，用心编标；
施璐德人，矢志领先。

Expect less and give us more,
Work hard, work hard, increasing the score,
Putting all our effort and heart we'll prepare tenders,
We'll exceed. We are Cnood members.

专注项目，倾情奉献；
商业计划，不复惹厌。
每时每地，沟通无限；
施璐德人，手握胜券。

Focused in projects, no material to store,
Business plans don't be a bore,
Whenever and wherever we interact with customers,
We'll succeed. We are Cnood members.

大势稳定，前所未见；
广揽项目，汇聚群贤。
客户心中，首屈一指；
施璐德人，手握胜券。

Certainties like never before,
More partners, more projects, demands galore
First in the minds of our customers
We'll succeed. We are Cnood members.

选择在施璐德工作的理由

我之所以接受施璐德公司的工作邀请，是因为它给了我一个机会，不只是作为一名员工，更是作为一个合作伙伴；通常，我愿意接受一种能允诺给我成长机遇的挑战。对我来说，这种认识，这种感觉，这种允诺，就叫作"施璐德"。

当 Dennis 向我发出邀请、说服我相信施璐德公司的时候，曾对我说过一番话，这番话我至今记在心里："我们的目标，就是成为一个大家庭，所有人都一起成长，同时又有钱可赚，能为客户创造价值。我们将变得强大，并且值得信赖。施璐德将在它所从事的领域预示未来发展。"这是一种独特的经验，Dennis 借此来阐释、表述其特别的"人生项目"概念；听了他的话，我也被吸引进去，说服自己这就是我要走的路。他说得很对。这条路现在是，而且将来还会是，我所要走的路。

对于成功而言，至关重要的是保持开心，并坚信自己所做的事是正确的。就长期而言，在心态和预期成果之间，有一种直接的关联。我正在不断努力以达到这个目标，从而向整个团队表明，他们把宝押在我身上就是选对了。

我们是一个大家庭，一家以"施璐德"为母体的公司。我们要不断努力，在客户的心目中占据首屈一指的位置。我们要加强团队协作，聚焦于公司的目标，包容大度，全情投入，尊重他人，当机立断，对自己的能力和主观能动性充满信心。专注，连贯性，坚持不懈，这是未来成功的关键所系。

天佑施璐德，永远永远！

Why did I choose to work at CNOOD?

I accept to work with Cnood because it gives me a chance to be a partner more than an employee and normally I follow a challenge who can promise me something that could allow me to grow. This knowledge, this feeling, this promise is called CNOOD for me.

I still have in my mind the words of Dennis when he invited me to believe in Cnood:*"Our objective is to be a family, growing all together in a profitable way, creating value for customers. We will be strong and reliable. Cnood will mark the future in what it does"*. It was a unique experience by which he defines, captures and defends his special "project of life" and with his message I got involved and convinced me that it was the way to go. He was not wrong. It is and will continue to be my way.

Be happy, be convinced in what I do, is vital to be success. There's a direct correlation between a state of mind and what should be my results in the long term basis. I am working hard to achieve it, demonstrating the whole team that they didn't make a mistake in betting on me.

We are, and we will be seen as, one family, one company under Cnood umbrella. We must work and work hard to be first in the minds of our customers. We must work as a team focusing on what Cnood wants with generosity, commitment, respect, decision and faith in our abilities and initiatives. Concentration, continuity and perseverance are the very essence of our future.

God bless Cnood ever!!

尼古拉斯
Nicolas Kipreos

尼古拉斯出生于一个希腊裔家庭，当初他们为谋求更好机遇而举家徙居智利时，可谓身无长物，唯有成功之渴望、自由之身心，以及他们的爱心和对天主计划的信德。此后，他与兄弟和两个姐妹在极为清晰的原则指引下长大成人，受到过良好的教育和道德的熏陶，养成了简朴的生活方式，心中充满无尽之爱。几家声誉卓著的机构培养陶冶了他，帮助他实现远大理想。1993年，他与帕特里夏结为伉俪，育有四个儿女（玛丽亚·赫苏斯、比森特、本哈明、华金），一家人其乐融融。他信仰虔诚，日进日新，对待同事，真诚友善，但对自己认定正确之事抑或更佳之策，则必为之争辩，不轻言放弃。恒守敬人之道，临事唯以信、爱、真。一以贯之者，宽以待人、严以求实。

他不怕犯错，但若因自己未做分内之事、未能恪尽职守而累及他人，则必心怀畏惧。在施璐德，他受到热情欢迎，颇感自在裕如。自觉有义务为公司服务，期待不久即可回报。

他的座右铭是："正面思考，积极主动，充满自信，信仰坚定，生活必将更为稳定，更多实干行动，留下更丰富的经历和成果。"

Nicolas is part of a family of Greeks that came to Chile looking for better opportunities, with nothing but their desire to succeed, their freedom, their love and faith in God's designs. Thus he was raised with his brother and two sisters with very clear principles, good education and morals, simplicity in the way of living and an infinite love. He was formed in establishments of great reputation that have allowed him to reach great ideals. He married Patricia in 1993 and has four children (Maria Jesus, Vicente, Benjamin and Joaquin) forming a happy family. Live his faith very close to God and the Blessed Virgin Mary, trying to improve every day, being honest and kind with his colleagues, but without giving up to defend what he believes is right or better, always with respect, doing things with conviction, care and true. He always push to be soft in people and hard in facts.

He is not afraid to make a mistake, but yes if he does not do what he should, if he affects someone by not doing his duty. He feels very comfortable at Cnood where he has been generously welcomed. Feel a debt to the company that expects to pay off soon.

His maximum thinking is "think positively and masterfully, with confidence and faith, and life become more secure, more fraught with action, richer in experience and achievement".

CNOOD 的魅力
The Charm of CNOOD

■ Tiger

2011年初的一个机缘，和老池在上海的一个咖啡厅相识，对我来说，是一见如故，是相见恨晚。在短短的交流中，仿佛找到了另一个自我，心中一直存在的关于职业、处事、存在的意义等思索，被老池的"共同利益论"给完整地呈现出来了，因为认同和共鸣，决意加入CNOOD，那是心灵的一种归属。

CNOOD源于老池的博士论文"共同利益论"，是其理念的践行应用，知行合一。对企业来说，"共同利益论"的核心理念是公司所追求的目标是利益相关者的共同利益最大化。在企业外部，把客户、供应商和服务商的利益放在公司利益之上；公司内部，成员利益在公司利益之上。公司要做的是创造价值，做增值服务。

At the beginning of 2011, I made the acquaintance of Dennis at a café in Shanghai by a lucky chance. For me, it felt as if we were old friends when we met for the first time, and I regretted that we didn't know each other earlier. During the short talk, I seemed to have discovered another self. My thoughts about occupation, philosophy of life, existence etc, which I had kept in mind for years, were presented in a perfect manner by Dennis' theory of "common interests". I decided to join CNOOD because of mutual identification. It was a belonging of soul.

The birth of CNOOD could be traced back to Dennis' doctoral dissertation "On Common Interests", as an application of the idea as well as a union of knowledge and practice. As for a company, the core idea of the theory is that it should seek the maximization of the common interests of all its stakeholders. Externally, a company should put the interests of clients, suppliers and service providers above its own interests; internally, it should put the interests

在"共同利益"为最高原则的指导下，使每个相关参与者的自主性、内心自发源动力、个人的潜能都能够得到充分的调动和发挥。一个内在动力被充分激发起来的个人、组织和群体是具有极其强大生命力和竞争力的，与此同时这个组织也将是一个积极向上的、友好的、利他的、充满关爱和情怀的组织。

蓦然回首，在CNOOD这个极具情怀的大家庭已走过了6个春秋，一起经历了非常多的壮举与震撼、见证一次次的突破和超越，心中存留无数次的激情与感动。往事历历在目，CNOOD一步步走过来，常常感觉不可思议，却是已成往事的CNOOD足迹。

在CNOOD，从无数的实际经历中，真正体会到，当我们面对客户、制造商和服务商时，什么是"信任"，什么是"尊重"，什么是"透明"，什么是"承诺"，什么是"责任"。

从CNOOD的工作氛围中，能真正感受到，什么叫"（无边的）乐观"，什么叫"人人平等"，什么叫"爱心"，什么叫"共同关心、创造开心"，什么叫"背对背工作

of its members above the interests of the organization. What a company should do is to create value and deliver value-adding services.

Guided by the supreme principle of "common interests", every stakeholder's initiative, its internal spontaneous motive power and its potentiality will be brought into full play. Any person, organization or group whose inner power is fully activated maintains exceptionally strong vitality and competitiveness. Meanwhile, the organization will be one that is vigorous, forward-looking, friendly, altruistic, filled with caring love and feelings.

Looking back, I suddenly realize that I have already been in the big family of CNOOD, which are full of feelings, for six years. Together we have experienced numerous feats and thrills, and have repeatedly witnessed breakthrough and surpassing, while deeply moved or brimming with passion for many times. I can picture all the past events vividly in my mind's eye, and often think it inconceivable that CNOOD comes all the way along step by step. However, this is the line of footprints that has become the past.

Working with CNOOD, I have truly understood, from various experiences when we face our clients, manufacturers and service providers, what "trust" is, what "respect" is, what "transparency" is, what "promise" is, and what "responsibility" is.

Only in the working atmosphere of CNOOD have I truly understood what "boundless optimism" is, what "equality for everyone" is, what "caring love" is, what "care

模式",什么叫"家国情怀"。

在这里,有不一样的思维,从开始的疑虑到逐渐认同,比如"做好一件事,什么事都能拿得起、放得下","做好一件事就是一念之间的事","每天锻炼一小时、学习一小时、冥思一小时"。

在这里,可以想"不敢想"的事情,可以做"不可能"的事情;在这里才体悟到什么叫"去中心化",什么叫"从心出发",什么叫"每个人都是CEO",什么叫"没有天花板",什么叫"鼓励学习"。

CNOOD是大家共同的平台,学习的平台,成长的平台,像磁铁一样聚集着越来越多的四海精英。CNOOD承载着一个远大的梦想,正前行在路上……

for each other and create delightfulness" is, what "back-to-back way of work" is, and what "patriotic complex" is.

Here, we have different ways of thinking, from the initial doubts gradually to identification, such as:"Do one thing right, and be able to take anything up or put it down"; "Doing a thing right is a thing within a moment"; "Every day, take exercise for an hour, study for an hour, and meditate for an hour."

Here, we are allowed to think about things that we "dared not think about", and do things that was "impossible". Here have I understood what "decentralization" is, what "starting from the heart" is, what "everyone as the CEO" is, what "no ceiling" is, and what "encouragement for learning" is.

CNOOD is a platform for everyone, a platform for learning and growth. It attracts like a magnet more and more elites from all over the world. CNOOD, with a big dream, is on its way going forward ...

丁林生
Tiger

丁林生,男,1974年生,1995年毕业于华东冶金学院冶金工程系金属材料与成型专业,1995—1998年于马鞍山钢铁股份有限公司任生产工艺与生产计划工程师,1998—2007年于泰国伟成发钢铁集团任工程师、生产部主管、工厂厂长。2007年回上海,从事钢铁行业国际贸易;2011年成为施璐德合伙人。

Born in 1974, Tiger graduated from the Department of Metallurgical Engineering, East China University of Metallurgy, majoring in metal materials and forming. He worked in Ma'anshan Iron & Steel Co., Ltd. as production process and planning engineer during 1995–1998, and later worked for Sahaviriya Steel Industries as engineer, production supervisor and plant manager. Back to Shanghai in 2007, he was engaged in international iron and steel trade. He joined CNOOD as a partner in 2011.

2016-CNOOD 印象
2016-CNOOD IMPRESSIONS

■ Tony

I. 2016-01-23

乌镇的梦

昨夜遇见她
在乌镇的梦里
忽然
我想起什么
我看着她
她问怎么
我想起来了
这是梦

A Dream in Wuzhen

/She came to my dream
/Last night in Wuzhen
/Suddenly
/I remembered something
/Staring at her
/"What's up?" she asked
/I realized that
/it was a dream

II. 2016-03-18

丽水行

CNOOD 不来
丽水的樱花不开
我爱你们
笑靥如花

A Trip in Lishui

/Cerasus in Lishui do not blossom
/until CNOOD's coming
/I love you
/with a smiling face
/like the blossom Cerasus

III. 2017-07-15

<table>
<tr><td>

毕　业

度尽劫波兄弟在
相逢一笑泯恩仇
毕业
是结束
还是开始

</td><td>

Graduation

/After all the vicissitudes we still brothers
/smiling off our old grudges when we meet again
/Graduation
/is it the end
/or a beginning?

</td></tr>
</table>

Yes, no matter where, when and how we still brothers, all we need is just a smile, graduation is more a beginning rather than an end.

IV. 2016-08-29

Johnson

告别 Johnson
从海门回上海
我却不知道
是归乡
还是离乡

Johnson

/Bidding farewell to Johnson,
/back to Shanghai I go, leaving Haimen.
/Yet I don't know
/whether I'm on my way home
/or leave home.

备注：Johnson 是只狗，作者也是只"狗"，漂泊。海门不是家，上海是家？此心安处是吾乡，告别 Johnson，到底是归乡，还是离乡？所以是 go home vs leave home，但是语法表达不知正确否。

V. 2016-09-15

归 途

竹杖轻胜马
芒鞋石头路
一钩新月破黄昏
万点明星光晕

Homeward Journey

/With a bamboo stick better than riding a horse
/I tread a stony road in straw sandals.
/At dusk, a crescent moon, hooked, pierces the sky;
/at night, a million bright stars twinkle.

备注：轻胜马，此处指芒鞋竹杖更轻快，实指内心轻松舒快，引自《定风波·莫听穿林打叶声》。

VI. 2016-09-29

墨 龙

性敏多慧下笔成
拂袖揽月射阳生

In Molong

/With an agile disposition and bright mind
/he produces a piece of writing the moment his brush pen is put to paper
/flicking his sleeves
/he is determined to pluck the moon in the sky

备注：此句是作者在墨龙钢管项目之旅清晨登上青州云门山，浮现在脑海的诗，此刻作者便是吴射阳，寄托情感。

VII. 2016-12-06

| 静 安 | Jing'an |

常随佛学　　　　　　　/Learn constantly from Buddha
福寿康宁　　　　　　　/and you will be endowed with happiness
心生　种种魔生　　　　 longevity, good health and peace
心灭　种种魔灭　　　　/All evils exist as long as the mind exists
　　　　　　　　　　　/and vanish as soon as the mind vanishes.

VIII. 2016-12-30

在巴黎

没有你
今天的感情
只是昨天的残壳
没有你
良辰美景更与谁说

In Paris

/Without you
/the feelings of today
/are but a empty fragment of yesterday.
/Without you,
/whom could I share the beautiful scenes in a fine moment?

IX. 2017-01-12

常熟日志

四季相续
光阴暗把流年度
人生渐往
追忆骑竹嬉游处

试问
常熟应不好
却道
此心安处是吾乡

Changshu Diary

/The four seasons alternate with each other,
/as time is fleeting quietly.
/Gradually life moves on,
/and I recollect childhood days when riding a bamboo stick as a toy horse.

/I ask myself tentatively,
/"But Changshu isn't that good, is it?"
/The reply:
/"My home is where my heart is at peace."

2016年，我加入CNOOD，在我眼里的CNOOD，无论你是想做一个业界精英、老板、企业家，或是哲学家、乞丐、诗人，都可以，在CNOOD，每个人都有无限的可能，在CNOOD，心有多远，就能走多远！

2017年，继续，寻梦……

I joined CNOOD in 2016. In CNOOD, as I see, you could be any kind of person, be it professional elite, boss, entrepreneur, or be it philosopher, beggar, poet—whatever. Everyone in CNOOD possesses infinite possibilities. Here, you can go as far as your heart goes.

In the year 2017, the dream-seeking journey will continue …

刘彬
Tony

刘彬，别名观棋柯烂，好古文，寄情于松桂云壑。毕业于上海大学，2016年加入施璐德。

Tony, aka "A Woodcutter Watching the Chess Game Long Ago", is fond of Chinese ancient proses and finds enjoyment in natural scenery such as "pine trees, sweet-scented osmanthus, and valleys shrouded in clouds". He graduated from Shanghai University and joined CNOOD in 2016.

人生如戏，CNOOD 是我的舞台
Life Is Like a Drama, and CNOOD Is My Stage

■ Sissi

1. 初识于五月天

第一个参与的项目是在施璐德装备制造（常熟）工厂制造的第一个项目。初始，我们刚到常熟港的时候还没有施璐德装备制造（常熟），我和四位同事一起到常熟6号库建厂。开始我对这个"建厂"并没有很清晰的概念，只觉是件光荣而艰巨的使命，作为一枚新人，自觉应该多听，多做事，勤思考。浩瀚大海中，即便一只小小的鱼，也要有掀起惊涛骇浪的豪情壮志；即便是黑夜中的渺小星辰，也能照亮星空，那是团结的魅力。

一眼望去，不像是故乡满目苍山翠竹，而是一望无际的平原，浑厚浓浊的江水。五月雨后的常熟，空气中淡淡的鱼腥味夹杂着泥土的气息，再晚些就是钢铁焊

1. In May We First Met

The first project I took part in since I joined CNOOD was also the first ever project carried out in the factory of CNOOD Equipment Manufacture (Changshu). In the beginning when we arrived at Port of Changshu, CNOOD Equipment Manufacture (Changshu) did not yet exist. My four colleagues and I came to Warehouse No.6, with the mission of building a factory. At first, I did not get a clear idea about "building a factory", and only considered it as a glorious but difficult task. As a new staff member, I thought I ought to listen more, practice more and think more. In the vast ocean, even small fish should have the ambition to cause terrifying waves; in the darkness of night, even tiny stars can light up the sky. This is the charm of unity.

Unlike the blue mountains and green bamboos meeting the eye on every side in my hometown, all that I could see were a boundless stretch of flatlands and the thick,

接味，但我们欣喜若狂，因为经过一番努力与改建，生产线已经开始正常运作。万事开头难，一个好的开始成功了一半。作为我第一个参与的项目，更多的是将之前在 work manual 中学到的采购跟单理论知识，亲身实战了一番。不积跬步，无以至千里；不积小流，无以成江海。从现场学习焊接防腐知识，到文件制作，从懵懵懂懂，到慢慢有所了解。

2. 英雄的灵魂伴我成长

荆州——霸主们的必争之地，滚滚长江穿城而过，护城河边古老的明清古城墙诉说着历史，人们耳熟能详的"大意失荆州"就发生在这里，一座有着雄厚文化和浓厚历史底蕴的古城。经过第一个项目的学习，大致明白一般项目都有哪些环节，每个角色负责哪些模块。相比之下，比执行第一个项目多了几分忐忑，有了些沉重的责任感，但也更加坚定、自信。每到一个地方执行项目，都能领略到不同的风土人情，第一天整装出行，途经宜昌，热情的司机师傅一路上讲述宜昌的各种历史故事，路过猇亭，夷陵之战描述得活灵活现，似乎他曾经参与其中。在沙市执行的项目

muddy water in the Yangtze River. After a May shower, faint smell of fish permeated the air in Changshu, mixed with the odor of mud, and later, the smell of the steel welding. We were overjoyed, because the production line was beginning to operate normally after a good effort and reconstruction. As the saying goes, "The first step is always difficult; well begun is half done." Since it was the first project I took part in, what I mainly did was to put into practical operation the knowledge of purchasing order, which I learned from the work manual. There is a famous saying by Xunzi, a great Chinese philosopher in 3rd century BC: "You cannot cover a thousand *li* without the accumulation of small steps; you cannot make a big river or a sea without the convergence of tiny creeks." From on-the-spot learning of welding corrosion protection to documentation, I have gradually become well-informed from being totally ignorant.

2. Growing up with Souls of Ancient Heroes

As a place of great strategic importance, the old city of Jingzhou is divided by the rolling flow of Yangtze River. Timeworn city walls built in the Ming and Qing dynasties stand beside the moat, as if telling stories about the past. It is an ancient city with profound historical and cultural background, where the famous story "Jingzhou Lost Due to Negligence" took place. Owing to the experience in the first project, we roughly understood the stages an average project would consist of, and the assignment of roles with their corresponding segments. Compared to the first project, we were more anxious

持续了两个多月，我和同事凝聚了深厚的革命友谊，开始的时候我们会一起负责一个事情，然后一起讨论。后来我们进行了分工，她主要负责焊接部分，我负责防腐部分。项目执行当中，当然会出现各式各样的困难险阻，我们互相帮助，互相关心，有时也会向前辈们寻求帮助。我们痛并快乐着，回首艰难岁月，却满心欢喜。这个项目带给我的，更多的是一种心智上的成熟，从学生到职场工作人的转变。

3. 天道酬勤

栉风沐雨，玉汝于成。刚开始客户只是一个口头的询价，和我多次强调不需要报价，只想了解一下市场价格水平，我还是给了详细的报价。同事在国外拜访时，仔细地回答客户提出的很多疑问，不久后，客户下单了。意外之喜，也许是天道酬勤吧。转战广州，前期在前辈们的指导下，我完成项目生产前的工作。第一次独自在一个陌生的城市跟项目，并且是一个新领

with a strong sense of responsibility, while at the same time more resolute and confident. Every time we arrived in a new city, we were able to have a taste of local conditions and customs. On the first day, we got ready and go on the trip. When in Yichang, our warm-hearted driver told us many historical stories all the way. Passing by Xiaoting, he gave a narration of the Battle of Yiling so vividly as if he had been in the battle himself. The project in Shashi lasted more than two months, during which time I developed a cordial friendship with my colleague. In the beginning, we were in charge of one task together, and had discussions with each other. Later, we divided up the duties: she was in charge of the welding part, and I the corrosion protection part. There were, of course, all kinds of difficulties and setbacks throughout the project cycle. We aided and cared for each other, sometimes seeking help from seniors. We have gone through pains and remain happy. Looking back on the hard times, we are yet filled with joy. What this project has brought to me most is the maturity of mind, while I have successfully transformed from a college student to a professional staff member.

3. God's Reward for Diligence

Working hard despite adverse circumstances helps you to reach success. At the very beginning, a foreign client made an oral inquiry, emphasizing repeatedly that he only wanted to find out the overall price level on the market and did not need formal quotation. However, I gave him a detailed quotation. My colleague called on the client and answered his questions carefully. Shortly

域的产品，又是一个新的挑战，一段新的体验。项目周期持续很长，几次往返广州，当中经历了种种，从给客户安排行程，到产品技术讨论、产品后期服务等。多重角色的扮演，方方面面，有进步，也有不足。感恩每一位给我指导，给予我灵感的良师益友。

4. 我在这里，眺望南美洲那一抹红

烈日炎炎，晴空万里，长江边上结构车间里火光四溅，向日葵般灿烂。钢结构生产如火如荼，我们的产品占据了大半个结构车间。钢结构不比钢管，结构复杂，做好一件事，什么事情都能拿得起放得下，只要自信，没有持久的困难，秉承这个原则，坚持往前走。公司安排了专业的QC部门同事驻场指导。我和Jenna一同负责两个项目，项目地点是巴拿马和多米尼加，都属于港建类的钢结构产品。项目管理中，主要在于对各个环节的掌控，我们的专业度即是考虑周到、全面。遇到问题，前辈给我们指导，自己跟随内心选择正确的解决办法。

after that, the client placed an order with us. It was a happy surprise, maybe God's reward for our diligence. Later, I was assigned a project task in Guangzhou, completing the pre-production work with the guidance from senior staff members. It was the first time that I carried out a project in a strange city all on my own. In addition, it involved products in a new field, and became a new challenge and experience for me. The project cycle was very long, during which I went to Guangzhou and back several times and experienced a lot of things, from schedule setting for the client to technical discussion about products and after-sale service. The multiple role playing involved various aspects and I made progress as well as showed shortcomings. I owe a deep gratitude to all the good tutors and worthy friends who have guided and inspired me.

4. I'm Here, Looking into Distance at that Touch of Red in South America

It was sunny all over the land under a scorching sun. The sparks were flying in all directions in the Structure Plant near the Yangtze River, as splendid as sunflowers. The production of steel structures was going on like a raging fire, and our products occupied more than half the space of the Structure Plant. Unlike steel tubes, steel structure products were more complicated. In order to do one thing right, you have to be able to take anything up or put it down. No difficulty will last long if you have confidence. We adhered to this principle and kept on moving forward. Professional colleagues from the QC Department were sent by our company to give us on-site guidance.

Jenna and I were jointly in charge of two projects, one in Panama and the other in the Dominican Republic, both of which involved steel structure products for port construction. In terms of project management, the main job was the control of every stage, and our professionalism lay in thoughtfulness and comprehensiveness. When facing a problem, we received directions from seniors while following the heart in choosing the correct solution.

在 CNOOD 工作两年，大家互相关心，创造开心，时刻感受到大家庭的温暖。人生如戏，未来，我们一起演好每一场戏，我的故事里有你们。

At every moment during my two years in CNOOD, I can feel the warmth of a big family whose members care for each other and create delightfulness. Life is like a drama. In the future, let's play every act of it successfully; every one of you is in my story.

吴茜
Sissi

Sissi：慢热，但适应能力强；怀旧，但不喜欢一成不变。内心情感坚韧炙热，但从不轻易释放。偏像双子的金牛座，一半稳重，一半分裂。

Sissi is a person who warms up slowly but with a strong ability to adapt to different circumstances; while nostalgic for the past, she does not like invariability. Though filled with firm, passionate sentiments, she never releases them rashly. She is a Taurus closer to Gemini, half steady and half schizophrenic.

峥嵘岁月
Uncommon Days

■ Lee Thompson

恰同学少年，风华正茂。

"感谢"二字，书面上已显苍白无力，唯有开心、关心和爱心，方能终成一家人。

至此，已进入施璐德一载，经历过痛苦和迷茫，但是每每如此，我都咬紧牙关，继续向前，结果往往会给我一个激励的答案，更多地，是收获了知识、经验和情谊，这些才是最珍贵的财富。

对每个人来说，未来都是光明的，希望我们可以一起努力，抓住机遇，为自己，为公司，创造一个更好的明天。

"So young were we then/in our best years of life."

The word "thanks" on paper appears pale and feeble. Only by joy, care and compassion can we be bound together as one family.

Now I have been with CNOOD for one year. Every time I underwent pains and confusions I would grit my teeth and continue to move forward. Often there would be an exciting answer waiting for me; what is more, I gained new knowledge, experience and friendship, which were my most valuable treasure.

Future is bright for everyone. I hope that we make joint effort and seize the opportunities, creating a better tomorrow for ourselves as well as for CNOOD.

姓名：李振宇
性别：男
生日：1992.07.23
星座：狮子座
毕业院校：哈尔滨理工大学、上海大学
专业：材料工程
入职年份：2016 年
爱好：篮球、舞蹈
座右铭：锲而不舍，金石可镂

李振宇
Lee Thompson

Name: Len Thompson
Sex: Male
Birthdate: July 23,1992
Zodiac Sign: Leo
Graduated from: Harbin University of Science and Technology, Shanghai University
Major: Materials Engineering
Year of Joining CNOOD: 2016
Hobbies: Basketball and dancing
Motto:Many strokes fell down strong oaks.

小白的梦想
The Dreams of a Rookie

■ Beny Wang

慈猴贺岁兴万象，金鸡报晓迎新春。在这辞旧迎新的时刻，回顾过去展望未来已成为每个施璐德成员的年终日常。

2016 年自认为一种巧合与 CNOOD 结缘，认识了大家庭的每一位成员，被她的温情所感化，被她的文化所吸引，被她的工作性质所痴迷。成员之间真诚以待相濡以沫，期盼的是彼此的茁壮成长。回想当初从一个懵懂无知的毕业小白，在她的呵护与培育下，上项目——培训——报价——跟客户——再培训，一路走来，混沌——清醒——再混沌——再清醒。虽然有些坎坷失落，但实实在在的充实和满足。

With the Monkey extending New Year's greetings, everything prospers; the Golden Rooster ushers in spring. It has become the routine task for every CNOOD member to look back upon the past and look forward to the future when we bid farewell to the old year and welcome the new one.

In 2016, I was connected with CNOOD by what I deemed a coincidence, and made the acquaintance of every member of this big family. Since then I have been moved by her tenderness, attracted by her culture, and infatuated with the nature of her business. Members treat each other with sincerity, help each other in times of need, and hope each other to grow strong. I can still recall how I was trained and nurtured by her when I was a totally ignorant rookie newly graduating from college: launching a new project, training, quotation, following up with clients, and re-training. I have come a long way, form confusion to soberness, then confusion and soberness again. Though I have undergone

2017年到来了,小白的梦想紧随新年的脚步不停歇。续过去一年的计划,小白将着手思想、语言和业务"三步同时走计划":

1. 思想

俗话说:思想的高度决定事业的高度。施璐德是个爱学习有内涵的企业,孔孟之道、阳明心学将成为我攻读的重点,目标:读好五本经典。人们常说:人从书里乖。书是精神的食粮,前进的动力,迷途的灯塔。"平常心"的磨炼除了实战,读书是另外一条绝好的途径,书能使人明事理,判是非。

setbacks and frustrations, I feel satisfied and completely free from worry.

We are now entering the year 2017, and my dream-seeking steps are ever going on with New Year's pace. To continue the annual plan of last year, I will set about a "Three-Steps-in-One" plan:

1. Thoughts

As the saying goes, "The height of your thoughts determines the height of your career." CNOOD is a cultured company that loves learning. I shall focus my reading on the teachings of Confucius and Mencius as well as Wang Yangming's philosophy of human mind, with the goal of thoroughly studying five classic works. It is often said that "books make men wise". They are food for the soul, the driving force of progress, and the lighthouse when you lose your way. In addition to practice, reading is another excellent way of cultivating "normal mentality". Books make men sensible, and enable them to distinguish right from wrong.

2. 语言

好的交流表达能规避误解，善于化解矛盾。主要从英语学习和沟通表达两方面着手：

a. 进阶日常和商务英语水平；

b. 更多地与同事交流，重点聊日常（自认缺乏聊日常能力）。

3. 业务

公司的发展，个人的生存离不开实实在在的项目支撑。引 Kevin Tong 的一句话："不想赚钱的公司是耍流氓。"

业务的发展将从三方面出发：

a. 在 Work-manual 和 Workbench 的指导下，继续熟悉市场—销售—采购的整体和个体的业务流程；

b. 系统研读五本贸易类的书籍，关注国内外政治和经济动向的网站；

c. 对于活跃的阿曼市场，继续推进 Dredger 和石油天然气管道类项目，重点推进 Reinforced Thermal Plastic (RTP) Pipe 和 GRE（Glass Reinforced Epoxy Filament Wound）Pipe。

对于埃及市场，在安全的法律条款、付款方式和可能的软条款的前提下，推进基础设施建设项目（如：屠宰生产线）。

2. Speeches

Good communication and expression help to avoid misunderstanding and eliminate conflicts. I will begin with two chief aspects: English learning; communication and expression.

a. Promotion of proficiency in both daily and business English;

b. More communication with colleagues, mainly talking about daily matters (an ability that I consider myself as lacking).

3. Business

True, dependable support of projects is crucial to the development of a company and the personal livelihood of all its members. To quote Kevin Tong, any company that doesn't aim to make money is a rogue.

Business shall be developed in three dimensions:

a. To get better informed, directed by Work-manual and Workbench, with overall and specific business processes of marketing, sales and procurement;

b. To read systematically five books on trade, while paying close attention to websites concerning political and economic trends both home and abroad;

c. As for the active market in Oman, to further advance dredger as well as oil and gas pipeline projects, with emphasis on Reinforced Thermal Plastic (RTP) Pipe and Glass Reinforced Epoxy Filament Wound (GRE) Pipe;

As for the market in Egypt, to advance infrastructure construction projects (e.g. slaughtering line), having taken into account legal articles, payment way and possible soft clauses.

对于阿拉伯联合酋长国和沙特阿拉伯市场，需要加大推进力度。

针对未来市场的业务，核心目标：实现一个具有真正施工（construction）的项目，打破只有E和P，没有C的局面。

相信理想很丰满，现实必然很骨感。小白已渐渐地长出了新芽，生了根，虽然还不能完全独立迎风浪顶风雪，但触角正在延伸、正在茁壮。

相信2017年的小白定成大白！

As for the markets in United Arab Emirates and Saudi Arabia, to make greater effort in advancing projects.

The core objective in terms of business in future market is to carry out one project with real "C" (construction), ending the situation where there are only "E" (engineering) and "P" (procurement) while "C" is missing.

Ideals are always believed to be full, while the reality is skinny. The rookie, however, has gradually put forth new buds and taken his roots. Though he is unable to face the waves and brave the storms by himself, his antenna is stretching to all sides, strong and sturdy.

I am convinced that the rookie is sure to become an expert in 2017!

王滔
Beny Wang

姓名：王滔
性别：男
学历：硕士
毕业学校：中国科学院上海硅酸盐研究所
兴趣爱好：羽毛球，唱歌和阅读
座右铭：伟人总是甘为卑微

Name: Beny Wang
Sex: Male
Degree: Master
Graduated from: Shanghai Institute of Ceramics, Chinese Academy of Sciences
Hobbies: Badminton, Singing & Reading
Motto: A Great Man Is Always Willing To Be Little!

A Partir del Corazón, Comienza el mundo

■ Dennis

A partir del 18 de septiembre de 2009, CNOOD ahora ya cumple su séptimo año. A lo largo de nuestro camino, encontramos cada vez más compañeros que comparten la misma visón con nosotros, empresarios que son muy arrogantes y emprendedores, y los trabajadores que persiguen sus sueños con mucha perseverancia; No obstante, los problemas también surgieron: tanto la gente presumidas con sus logros y su ambiente seguro, como los conflictos entre los miembros. Entonces, ¿cómo es la situación actual de CNOOD, cuales son muestras metas, qué es la estrategia de desarrollo y cómo lo llevamos a la práctica?

Hace ocho años, CNOOD nació como un infante, con tan solo cinco personas: Fei Feng, la madre de Fei Feng, el niño de Fei Feng, Wen Tao, y yo(Dennis). Kevin Tong y Shirley no estaban, pero nos apoyaban como siempre. Cada uno llevabamos las siguientes palabras estampadas en el corazón, que son: amor, ambición, confianza, y tranquilidad.

En el julio de 2009, CNOOD firmó su primer contrato, el cliente fue SALZGITTER; en el octubre, cerró el primer contrato con TOTAL NIGERIA; y el noviembre, con THYSSENCRRUB VIETNAM.

En agosto de 2010, Jet particpó en nosotros. En marzo, el primer contrato con CUNADO fue firmado. El abril, se celebró el primer acuerdo con GEONET GROUP y el julio, primer negocio cerrado con ARCELORMITTAL. Al fin del año, Shirley oficialmente dimitió a la empresa por causas de familia y su desición sobre carrera profesional.

El febrero de 2011, Ahuan vino; en marzo y agosto, vinieron Tiger y Tina Jiang; en octubre, incorporó Wendy. En mayo, se iniciarón una serie de cooperaciones con Juan Gabriel; y gracias al empeño de Kevin, CNOOD ganó en agosto su primer proyecto a neviel de diez mil toneladas, que fue concluido en octubre del mismo año.

El enero de 2012, Fay incorporó. Hasta ese momento/aquel entonces?, las

estructuras funcionales de la empresa fue básicamente establecidas. En mayo, comenzó la cooperación con GSL, el mismo mes incorporó Amir. En junio, cormtemos la cooperación con Jet, y en octubre, Joy vino.

El abril de 2013, el proyecto PDVSA concluyó con todo éxito después de un año de trabajo.; el octubre, se terminó la cooperación con Joy.

En enero de 2014, incorporaron Mario, Nico, Cristian y Gino, CNOOD LATAM S.P.A se puso en marcha sus actividades entonces. En febrero, celebró su primer contrato con IMI. En marzo, incorporó Tina Xu. En mayo, el proyecto de IMI terminó con éxito. El mismo mes, la fábrica de Changshu inició sus operaciones. El junio, firmó el primer contrato con SKYWARD. En julio, Wael participó. En agosto, primer contrato con HUTA MARINE fue confirmado. En agosto, incorporó Neo. En septiembre, conmenzó el primer negocio con SUEZ CANAL. En octubre, unió Pat, y en deciembre, CNOOD HK LTD se creó.

En enero de 2015, CNOOD firmó el primer contrato con BELFI, y en marzo, con YPFB. En junio vino Chin, luego en septiembre vino Esteban. En septiembre, CNOOD ENGINEERING S.P.A se estableció.

En enero de 2015, CNOOD ganó su primer negocio sobre el producto de estructura metálica. En junio, incorporó Ben, asímismo, Paul en julio, y Tina Zhang en diciembre. Hasta este momento, la disposición global del mercado se ha establecido preliminariamente, abarcando sus necogios en las areas de: Petróleo y gas, Minería, Agua, Energía Renovable e Infraestructura.

(ilustración)

Nuestro camino nunca ha sido fácil. Cualquier desición, se debe tomar con mucho precaución como si fuera una persona caminando sobre el hielo. La mayoría de las veces, lo único que podíamos hacer es seguir la intuición del corazón, por falta de experience que nos pudiera apoyar. Durante tal proceso, practicamos más, pensamos más, y aprendemos más, porque el hombre que pretende verlo todo con claridad antes de decidir nunca decide. Además, cortemos las relaciones sin vacilar con gente que tuviera problemas morales; y corregimos los errores por más frecuente que se encontraran. De tal modo, aprendemos a base de los discubrimientos, y avanzamos a base de las perseguimientos.

El mejoramiento de los negocios depende a la máxima bondad y la máxima sinceridad. Sólo con llevar la bondad siembre en las prácticas del trabajo, se mantendrá la carrera a lo largo del tiempo, y sólo con ser sincero a la gente, se les conmoverá y les apasionaná profundamente. La bondad máxima y la sinceridad máxima no se miden con medidas. Por eso, no piensan que ninguna virtud sea trivial, y así la descuiden; no piensen que cualquier vicio sea trivial, y así lo practiquen. El mucho se acumula desde pequeño, la montaña se empieza por la tiera; la virtud es el destino de la bondad. I Ching("Libro de las Mutaciones") dice: El movimiento del cielo sigue su propio principio, así un caballero debe aprovechar los oportunos para ser fuerte incesantemente; la tendencia de la tierra también es riguroso, así un caballero la debe obedecer siempre para apoyar los demás con sus virtudes.

¿La carrera de la bondad máxima requiere muchas aportaciones? No, ello depende solo a las cualidades morales: compasión, lealtad, cortesía, sabiduría y compromiso, que son las cualidades bien conocidas y admiradas por todo el mundo. Si las llevamos en práctica efectivamente, los compañeros vendrán para cooperar con nostros, la gente se acumularán para apoyarnos, y nuestra carrera llagará a la prosperidad. Si la gente solo admiran los vencedores y desprecian los vencidos, la situación es nada más el tanefímero como las nubes pasajeras; hasta que la gran muralla construida por Qin Shi Huang (Emperador chino en Dinastía Qin), tampoco es un logro eterno. Sino solo la virtud y el moral de Confucio y Mencio trascenden a lo largo de la historia y benefician a todos.

No es buena idea trabajar de una manera forzada, de obedecer a ciegas, ni de engañar. Como lavar arenas, los oros son los que se sedimentan al final; a lo largo de la historia, solo la bondad máxima y la sinceridad máxima traspasan de generación a generación. Su influencia hacia la gente es como la penetración de la lluvia en la tierra, tan silenciosa pero profunda. Ganando el apoyo de la gente con la máxima bondad posible, así se encuentran las oportunidades; tratando los demás con la máxima sinceridad posible, así se extienden las posibilidades. Aprovechando las oportunidades, consiguimos las metas; extendiendo las posibilidades, prosperamos nuestros logros.

El desarrollo de las cosas depende de cómo lo hace una persona. La persona y su voluntad es la clave fundamental del éxito o del fracaso. ¿Qué es la voluntad? Es un corazón lleno de amor, es decir, educar la gente con amor, tratar los demás con amor, y hacer las cosas con amor. Amar a la gente, significa exigirte mucho a ti mismo y esperar poco de los demás, así te ahorrarás disgustos y luego se puede esperar la llegada del éxito. Con respecto al factor humano, se considera fundamental trabajar en equipo. La creación de un equipo es una misión de toda la vida, en la que beneficiamos en trabajar con la gente de diferentes edades: observando a los niños, aprenderemos sus pensamientos tan puros e inocentes sin el menor pecado; trabajando con los compañeros adultos, sus esfuerzos y empeños son tan energéticos que nos ayudan eliminar cualquier obstáculo en el camino; aprendiento con los mayores, nos enriquecen con sus experiencias abundantes y consideraciones más prudentes gracias a los años acumulados. No importa el tamaño de la empresa, lo que cuenta es la voluntad de trabajar juntos y la fraternidad entre sí, con lo que se maximiza las fortalezas de cada integrande, sacando lo mejor de sí y complementándolo con las de los demás. Sin el mismo espíritu, nos llevará nada más un resultado mediocre por más personas y recursos que tengamos disponibles. Por lo tanto, creamos grupos de pequeño tamaño con menos jerarquía pero con más fraternidad, establecemos estructuras más flexibles que adapte a diferentes casos, así podemos esperar grandes resultados.

El emprender es un camino donde unimos la gente, sus esfuerzos y sus voluntades. Si conseguimos estos claves, y con un poco de paciencia, el éxito será solo una questión de tiempo. Espero que siempre mantenguen una mentalidad positiva por lo bien y por lo mal de su entorno. El espíritu emprendedor tiene que basarse en una fé solida, tener una vista pionera e iniciar nuevos negocios constantemente. Entonces, los pasos avanzan sin cesar, y las habilidades cada día suben a otro nivel. El tiempo de nuestra vida es tan emífero y valioso, si tardamos mucho en preocuparnos en los posibles fracasos o vacilamos demasiaso para tomar las desiciones, ¿cómo podemos tener tiempo para dedicarnos en las acciones exitosas?

CNOOD, es efectivamente una roca firme en la que construyen la casa; una plataforma sobre la que inician las carreras novedosas; y una familia donde encuentran compañeros para compartir los sueños. Comporte siempre con un corazón sincero, estoy cnovencido de que ustedes serán un equipo tan fuerte como el acero, encontrarán compañeros de toda la vida, y fundarán la base sólida para la carrera del futuro. Si quieren ganar apoyo de los demás, primero hay que ser una pauta de sí mismo. Piense en lo que piensan los demás como si fuera su propio reto; busque soluciones para los demás como si fuera su propio problema; y ponga en situación de los demás como si fuera a entorno de sí mismo. Trate a sus congéneros igual que quisiera ser tratado. Exigirse mucho a si mismo y esperar poco de los demás. De ese modo, esperamos sacar un resultado maravilloso de los negocios.

Por favor, dedíquense diez años a CNOOD, les aseguramos un futuro total diferente y un equipo invencible.

Apartir del corazón, estamos en el camino de emprender.

池勇海,男,汉族,1970年出生于湖北仙桃。先后毕业于武汉理工大学、复旦大学,获管理学硕士学位、经济学博士学位。

他是一名跨国公司的创立人、执行董事。他致力于构筑一个平台,打造一个共创、共享、共治的无边界的有机生态系统。让每一位在这个平台上的国内外合伙人、员工都能在这里成长、壮大成为未来的CEO。

他也是一个"屌丝",上演了一场真正的屌丝逆袭。从农村里走出来的孩子,羞涩,不自信,哑巴英语到国际谈判中的从容、睿智、优雅的转身。

他是一个造梦者,他告诉身边的每一个人,无论你是想做一个业界精英、老板CEO或是哲学家、诗人、乞丐都可以。心有多远,你就能走多远!

他更是一个履梦人,为了实现自己的"中国梦",先后造访了乌克兰、德国、伊朗、叙利亚、印度尼西亚、智利、澳大利亚、伊拉克、美国、土耳其、厄瓜多尔、尼日利亚、印度、埃及、沙特、巴拿马、玻利维亚等数十个国家。他用他的双脚丈量着世界,也用他的梦想为中国制造与中国创造走向世界贡献自己的力量。

Born in Xiantao, Hubei Province in 1970, Dennis Chi is of Han nationality and graduated from Wuhan University of Technology with a master's degree in Management Science and from Fudan University with a doctoral degree in Economics.

He is the founder and executive director of a multinational company, devoting himself to building a platform and an organic ecosystem without boundary, which is created, shared and managed by all its members, so that every partner, domestic or foreign, as well as every employee, can grow stronger to become a future CEO.

He used to be a "loser"; however, he performed a real counterattack. Once a shy, unconfident boy from the countryside with extremely poor English speaking proficiency, he has transformed into a business leader who shows calmness, wisdom and grace in international negotiations.

He is a dream-maker who tells everyone around him: "You could be any kind of person, be it professional elite, boss, CEO, or be it philosopher, poet, and beggar— whatever. You can go as far as your heart goes!"

He is also a dream-fulfiller who, in order to realize his "Chinese Dream", has visited dozens of countries: Ukraine, Germany, Iran, Syria, Indonesia, Chile, Australia, Iraq, USA, Turkey, Ecuador, Nigeria, India, Egypt, Saudi Arabia, Panama, Bolivia, etc. He measures the world with his feet, and with his dreams he makes contribution to pushing Chinese manufacture and Chinese creation to the world.

池勇海
Dennis

自由而无用的灵魂——CNOOD 自序
Free and Useless Souls—Preface to CNOOD Yearbook

■ Dennis

CNOOD，为自由而生，为公平而生，为尊重而生，为关心而生，为互爱而生，为透明而生，为信任而生，为发展而生，为创造而生，为我们喜欢的未来而生；为少有所依而生，为青有所学而生，为老有所养而生；为中国的家人而生，为南美的家人而生，为西班牙的家人而生，为我们所有的家人而生；我们创造良好的发展环境，创造我们赖以生存的新天地。

CNOOD was born for freedom, fairness, respect, care, mutual love, transparency, trust, development, creation, and the future that we like. It was born for a community in which children have the means for their growing up, young people have opportunities to learn, and the aged are properly provided for. It was born for the families in China, the families in South America and those in Spain—all the families of ours. We create good environment for developing, as well as a new world upon which our livelihood depends.

CNOOD 的缘起

1. 关于个人的发展阶段

师父引进门，修行在个人。个人的发展，首先在于自己的努力，不是做样子，也不是装样子，而是实实在在，踏踏实实。不管是哪个阶段，莫不如是。个人的发展，也不可能是一帆风顺的。顺境，是经历；逆境，是经验，是难得的经验。没有必要，顺境的时候，忘乎所以；更没有必要，逆境的时候，肝肠寸断。去人欲，存天理；

About the Origin of CNOOD

1. About the Phases of Personal Development

As the saying goes, "The master initiates the apprentices, but their success depends on their own efforts." Personal development depends primarily upon one's effort—not making a show nor putting on an act, but being honest, steadfast and dependable. It is true with any phase of personal development. The road of personal development could not

致良知，事上练。此心光明，亦复何言。

每个人的喜好各不相同，每个人的起点各型各色，每个人的领悟侧重不一，每个人的发展轨迹也会是色彩斑斓，千差万别。起始三个阶段：基础建设阶段、方向遴选阶段、确定发展阶段。初步的发展将为以后的发展奠定人力、智力和财力基础。这要求学会终端服务。

我们需要的是有魄力的人，不是胆小如鼠的人；是敢于承担风险的人，不是逃避风险的人；是愿意为大家付出的人，不

be smooth all the time. To be in favorable circumstances is an experience; to be in adverse circumstances is a rare experience of trial. It is unnecessary to lose your head when in favorable circumstances; it is even more so to be heartbroken when in adverse circumstances. Remove human desires and cherish heavenly principles; obtain innate knowledge by practical exercise. If I'm upright and guileless in mind, what else do I have to say?

Everyone has his liking, with his unique starting point and level of understanding. Their paths of development are also multicolored with immense variety. The initial three phases include infrastructure, direction selecting and determination, laying the foundation for further development in terms of human, mental and financial resources. Learn and master the terminal service.

What we need are people who are bold and resolute, not those who are chicken-hearted; people who dare take risks, not those

是专门利己的人。

2. 关于我们的生存和发展环境

我们每个人都在创造自己生存的环境。和，则百生；斗，则全败。一粒老鼠屎，搞坏一锅羹。只要个别人做不利于团结的事情，不利于公司的事情，公司就很难有有利的发展环境，在严酷的竞争中必然落败。公司的发展，需要每个人共同来努力；公司的发展环境，需要每个人共同来创造；良好的发展氛围，需要每个人共同来维护。

我们提倡正能量的公开沟通交流。我们不是同事，是一家人。家人之间，互相包容、互相成全、互相成就，理所应当。难免有不理解的事情，正常沟通就行；有不能接受的事情，公开讲出来就好。有缘分走到一起，就是为一大事来，做一大事去。

我们反对负能量的私下沟通。耍心眼，搞内斗，结帮派，包藏祸心，都是属于不讲信用、为 CNOOD 所摒弃的人。坚持这种歪风邪气的人，第一时间就会为 CNOOD 所抛弃。在社会上的几乎所有的单位，负能量的东西大行其道，看起来理所应当。但是，在 CNOOD，不行。别人

who avoid them; people who are willing to work for the benefit of all, not those who consider only their own interests.

2. About Our Environment for Survival and Development

Every one of us is creating for himself an environment for survival. Form peace would all benefit; in fighting would all lose. As the saying goes, "One ill weed mars a whole pot of pottage." A company can hardly have a favorable environment for developing and will surely be defeated in fierce competition even if only few members of it do things detrimental to unity and the company. The development of a company needs the effort of all its members; its environment for developing needs to be created by all its members; and the atmosphere for developing needs to be maintained by all its members, too.

We encourage open communication with positive energy. We are more than colleagues; we are a family. It is reasonable that family members ought to forgive each other, help each other to achieve their goals, and fulfill each other. It is natural that there are things you cannot understand; just communicate as normal. If there are things you cannot accept, just say openly. Fortune has driven us together for a lofty ideal and the accomplishment of a great cause.

We oppose, however, private communication with negative energy. Exercising one's wits for personal gains, participating in internal strife, ganging up and harboring evil intentions—these are all untrustworthy behaviors that are rejected by CNOOD. People with these unhealthy practices will be soon cast aside by

都这样做，我们不一定这样做；别人都不这样做，我们也不一定不这样做。我们会按照事情本身需要的方式去做事情。

CNOOD 现在的内部发展环境相当不错，我们有关心公司发展的董事，形成心系新人成长的良好氛围，打造了互相关心的和谐文化。请不要在最好的环境里浪费自己的青春！

希望每个 CNOOD 人都能够自觉维护我们来之不易的良好的生存和发展环境，并尽自己的力量创造更好、更靓丽、更明媚的环境，争做 CNOOD 的脊梁。

关于我们的工作模式：基本架构、国外客户、当地合伙人、上海支持合伙人、支持高级经理、支持经理、支持助理。当地合伙人主要负责当地市场和采购，支持合伙人为当地合伙人提供各种支持。

关于 CNOOD 风险控制体系：我们的风险控制体系为六步法：（1）助理、经理、高级经理以及合伙人；（2）项目主管合伙人；（3）项目采购合伙人；（4）融资支持体系；（5）后台支持体系；（6）财务支持体系。

CNOOD. It seems natural that within almost all organizations in the society, things with negative energy are rampant. But it is not the case with CNOOD. It is not necessary for us to do what other people all do; neither is it necessary for us not to do what no one else does. We do anything in a way that is required by the thing itself.

CNOOD now has a very good internal environment for developing. We have directors of board who are concerned about the company's development, and have formed a good atmosphere for the growth of new members as well as a culture of harmony in which we care for each other. Please don't waste your best years of youth in the best environment!

I hope that every CNOOD member will consciously safeguard our hard-earned environment for survival and development, and do our best to make it better, brighter and more attractive. Every one of us shall be the backbone of CNOOD.

About our way of work: The underlying architecture involves foreign clients, local partners, supporting partners in Shanghai, supporting senior managers, supporting manages, supporting assistants. Local partners are responsible for local marketing and procurement, while supporting partners provide various supports for local partners.

About the risk management system: We have a risk management system with six components/steps: (1) assistants, managers, senior managers and partners; (2) project managing partners; (3) project procurement partners; (4) financing support system; (5) back

关于 CNOOD 的信仰：高尚的道德情操，坚强的意志，无比的自信心，自由而无用的灵魂。

关于我们的发展：什么是最长久的？帮助人。

关于我们个人：作为一个为追求真理而做学问的人，作品能否传世非常重要。我没有能力改变世界。依我建议的我当然高兴，不依我的也无所谓。名头是什么我历来不管，但作品或思想能传世，数十年来我是不断地争取的。（此为张五常语）

责任感、使命感、荣誉感

"记住你即将死去"是我一生中遇到的最重要箴言。它帮我指明了生命中重要的选择。因为几乎所有的事情，包括所有的荣誉、所有的骄傲、所有对难堪和失败的恐惧，这些在死亡面前都会消失。我看到的是留下的真正重要的东西。你有时候会思考你将会失去某些东西，"记住你即将死去"是我知道的避免这些想法的最好办法。你已经赤身裸体了，你没有理由不去跟随自己内心的声音。

什么叫文化中心？ 文化中心就是全世界的文化创造者都集中并发布文化成果的地方。与公元 7 世纪的长安相比，19 世纪的巴黎和现在的纽约还有一个缺点，就是缺少诗意。长安那可是充满了诗意，晚上

end support system; (6) accounting support system.

About the faith of CNOOD: high morals; strong will; incomparable confidence; free and useless souls.

About our development: What lasts the longest? Helping people.

About ourselves: As a scholar in pursuit of truth, I deem it of great importance whether my works will be handed down to future generations. I'm not able to change the world. If people listen to my advice, of course I will be happy; if they don't, it makes no difference to me. I never cared about the titles, but I have been striving unceasingly in the past decades for my works or thoughts to be handed down to future generations. (By Zhang Wuchang)

Senses of Duty, Mission and Honor

"Remember that you are going to die" is the most important maxim I have ever encountered in my life to help me make the big choices in life. Because almost everything, including all honors, all pride, all fear of embarrassment or failure, just vanish in the face of death. What I see then is truly important things that are left. Remember that you are going to die is the best way I know to avoid the trap of thinking you have something to lose. You are already naked. There is no reason not to follow your heart.

What is a cultural center? A cultural center is a place where cultural creators from all over the world assemble, presenting to the public the fruits of their work. Paris in the 19th century and New York in present day

是宵禁，宵禁不是为了战争而是为了管理秩序，108个坊，坊门关了，人只能在坊里面活动。所以下午就很重要了，有很多很多酒吧，这些酒吧都是来自中亚，即现在的哈萨克斯坦、吉尔吉斯斯坦的那些国家的漂亮女孩——胡姬开的。

而且文化创造者使命当中也有一个分工：希腊哲学家主要是考虑人和物的关系，印度哲学家主要是考虑人和神的关系，中国哲学家主要是考虑人和人的关系。

（1）模块化改革；
（2）旅级别指挥中心；
（3）指挥协同中心；
（4）专业化、协调、协同；
（5）团队；
（6）风险；
（7）关系；
（8）运营；

曾国藩曾说："轻财足以聚人，律己足以服人，量宽足以得人，身先足以率人。"其意为疏财能够团结人，严于律己能够使人信服，宽以待人能够得到人心，身先士卒能够领导众人。

问禅师："人的一生哪一天最重要？"禅师不加思索答道："今天。""为什么？"

have a common shortcoming compared with Chang'an in the 7th century, that is, lack of poetic flavor. Chang'an, on the contrary, was very poetic. Curfews were enforced then, not because there was a war, but for the purpose of maintaining order. There used to be 108 *fang*, or blocks in the city. When night fell, gates of the blocks were shut, and people's activities were confined within the blocks. As a result afternoon became even more important. At that time, there were many wine shops run by pretty girls from where are now Middle Asian countries such as Kazakhstan and Kyrgyzstan.

And there was a division of labor between them: Greek philosophers mainly considered the relation between man and object, Indian philosophers mainly considered the relation between man and God, while their Chinese counterparts mainly considered that between man and man.

(1) Modulation reform;
(2) Brigade-level command center;
(3) Command coordination center;
(4) Specialization, alignment and coordination;
(5) Team;
(6) Risks;
(7) Relations;
(8) Operation.

Zeng Guofan said, "If you are generous in aiding people, you can unite them; if you are strict with yourself, you can convince others; if you are lenient towards others, you can win their heart; if you charge at the head of your men, you can be their leader."

Someone asks a Zen master, "What's the most important day in a man's life?" Without

"因为今天是我们拥有的唯一财富。昨天不论多么值得回忆和怀念，它都像沉船一样沉入海底了；明天不论多么辉煌，它都还没有到来；而今天不论多么平常，它都在我们手里，由我们支配。"——珍惜今天，活在当下。

不要在该奋斗的年纪选择去偷懒，只有度过了一段连自己都被感动了的日子，才会变成那个最好的自己。

人，要么在读书，要么去旅行。身体和灵魂，必须有一个在路上。

让引力来做事情，用习惯来做事情。引力，是核心。

我：为什么我得不到机会？

Workbench：那是因为你没有把我造得很好。

我：是吗？

Workbench：自从你把我造出来以后，你甚至都不信任我。这也就意味着你连自己都不信任。

我：我会把你造得更完美。

Workbench：你得到的，将会远超你想要的。

科技的终极目标是什么，等科技做到极致，会发现，人文才是它最终极的目的地。码农再能干，可惜他们不会编制梦，他们只会造公路，造房子，搞装修。帮人造梦这种事，当然要交给文化工程师们来做了。

hesitation, the master answered, "Today." "Why?" "That's because today is the only wealth in our possession. Yesterday, however full of memories, has gone to the bottom of the sea like a sunken ship. Tomorrow, however splendid, has not arrived yet. Today, however common, is in our own hands and at our disposal."—So, treasure the time of today and live in the present moment.

Don't choose to be lazy at the age when you ought to make a good effort. You can the best person you could be only if you have had times that would move even yourself.

A man is either reading or going on a trip. One of the two—body and soul—must be on the road.

Let things be done by gravity, and do things by habits. Gravity—it is the core.

I: Why don't I have chance?

Workbench: You do not make me well.

I: Really?

Workbench: You even do not trust me since you make up me. It means that you do not trust you.

I: I will make up you perfect.

Workbench: You will have much more than you want.

What is the ultimate objective of science and technology? When science and technology have developed to the utmost, you'll find that humanity is ultimate destination. It's a pity that coding peasants, no matter how capable, are unable to weave dreams. All that they can do are building roads and houses and fitting them up. Things like helping people to make dreams, of course

所以，这篇文章，脑洞开得有点大。不过，既然开脑洞，不如开得越大越好。因为科技的进步，越来越快了。社会的发展被它带着向前狂奔，也越来越快。快得用理解力追不上，只能插上想象力的翅膀。任何时候都是如此：想象力，比知识更重要。 未来十年的社会和经济发展图景，将会切换到一个全新的操作系统。而设计和开发这个全新操作系统所用的语言，一个是科技，一个是万物互联，一个是文化。

失去一个客户只要三秒，得到一个客户的信任也许需要3年，买卖只是起点，服务没有终点。交易是小，做人是大，一旦达成合作，便永远是朋友。——被信任是一种快乐！

中华文明历经沧桑，从未间断，关键在于"己所不欲，勿施于人"。

作为CNOOD之CEO的素养：

（1）做人的素养；
（2）业务素养；
（3）如何对待吵架；
（4）如何对待郁闷；

then, are to be entrusted to cultural engineers.

So far in this essay, I have displayed a little bit of wild fantasy. However, since it involves fantasies, the wilder, the better. The progress of science and technology is getting increasingly more rapid, leading the society to gallop forward at an ever-faster pace. It is so fast that we cannot catch up by our understanding, and should use imagination instead. Imagination is always more important than knowledge. The image of socio-economic development in the coming decade will be switched to an entirely new operation system, the languages employed in the design and development of which include: first, science and technology; second, the internet of things (or universal connectivity); third, culture.

It takes only three seconds to lose a client, but three years to gain his trust. Buying and selling are but a start, while there is no end to our service. What kind of person you are is more important than what deal you are making. Anyone who has once become our client is our friend forever. It is joyful to be trusted!

Having gone through many vicissitudes, the journey of Chinese civilization has never been interrupted. The key lies in the maxim "Don't do unto others what you would not want done unto you."

The capabilities needed to be CEO of CNOOD:

(1) Personal qualities
(2) Business competencies
(3) The way dealing with quarrels
(4) The way dealing with depression

（5）与竞争者的关系；
（6）永不抱怨；
（7）积极，积极，再积极；主动，主动，再主动，做好自己生活的CEO；

（8）识人、用人。

启示：即使有些问题看起来真的是疯狂，但是有时候它还是真的存在；如果我们每次在看待任何问题都秉持着冷静的思考去找寻解决的方法，这些问题将看起来会比较简单。所以碰到问题时不要直接就反应说那是不可能的，而没有投入一些真诚的努力。

己所不欲，勿施于人！

做每件事情，让自己最满意！

真正的学生是要去学习、研究、探索、发问的，也不是不再年轻就结束了学习，而是要终其一生学习。只要你在学习，你就一定有老师，因为万事万物都是你的老师，叶片的风中飞舞、河水的喃喃细语……

站好自己的舞台；
站好自己的讲台。
唯有了解祖先的根源，
了解祖先的遭遇，
才知进退依据。
纪念长征，
为谁出发，
感受他们信仰的力量，
智慧的力量，
不相信权利的力量。
所有的真爱，都是为了更好地分离；不是为了得到。

(5) The relation with competitors
(6) Never complain
(7) Being positive and more positive; being proactive and more proactive; being the CEO of one's own life

(8) Identification and selection of talents

Inspiration for us: Certain problems, though seeming crazy, sometimes do exist. If we think calmly and seek the solution every time we face a problem, they will become less difficult. Therefore, don't react automatically saying "That's impossible!" before you have made some genuine effort.

Don't do unto others what you would not want done unto you!

Do everything and make yourself the most satisfied!

A true student is one who is prepared to study, research, explore and raise questions, without stopping it when no longer young, but keeping on during the lifetime. You do not necessarily have a teacher so long as you are studying, for all things in the universe are your teachers: falling leaves dancing in the wind, the murmuring of the river streams ...

Stand firm on the stage of your own;
Stand firm on the podium of your own.
We shall know when to advance and when to retreat/ only if we understand the roots of our forefathers / and their bitter experiences.
Commemorate the Long March/ and remember whom they were departing for. / Feel their strength of faith/ and of wisdom/ instead of believing in the strength of power or authority.
All genuine love is meant for a better parting, not for getting.

真正的教育是教导你"如何"去思考，而不是教你去思考些"什么"。如果你知道如何思考，如果你真的有那种能力，你就是一个自由的人。如果你能从教条、盲信、形式等当中解脱出来，你就会进一步发现它的真相。

一个真正强大的人，不会把太多心思花在取悦和亲附别人上面。所谓圈子、资源，都只是衍生品。最重要的是提高自己的内功。只有自己修炼好了，才会有别人来亲附。自己是梧桐，凤凰才会来栖；自己是大海，百川才来汇聚；花香自有蝶飞来。你只有到了那个层次，才会有相应的圈子，而不是倒过来。

突现，居然出现在经济里，突现的网红经济现象。

宇宙学里也有突现，简单原理叠加以后，越来越多的时候，就会有突现。

用模式做事情，让习惯做事情。

微小的差异，决定未来的方向。

What education is really about is instructing you "how" to think, instead of teaching you "what" to think. If you know how to think and really have that ability, then you are free. If you can extricate yourself from the shackles of dogma, superstition and formalism, you'll further discover their true colors.

A man who's truly strong will never bother to ingratiate himself with, or try to be close to and depend on others. The "circles" and "resources" are but byproducts. The most important thing is to enhance your innate capabilities. Only when you have accomplished perfect training will people try to be close to and depend on you. Only a phoenix tree attracts phoenixes to perch on it, and only the great sea receives the inflow of all rivers. If the flowers are fragrant, butterflies will naturally come. You will have corresponding circles only when you have reached the level, but not conversely.

It is a surprise that the catastrophe theory now could be applied to the economic field, i.e. the "Internet celebrity economy" emerging all of a sudden.

The concept "catastrophe" is also found in cosmology. When simple factors pile up increasingly, there will be a catastrophe.

Do things by mode, and let things be done by habits.

Tiny differences determine the direction of the future.

池勇海，男，汉族，1970年出生于湖北仙桃。先后毕业于武汉理工大学、复旦大学，获管理学硕士学位、经济学博士学位。

他是一名跨国公司的创立人、执行董事。他致力于构筑一个平台，打造一个共创、共享、共治的无边界的有机生态系统。让每一位在这个平台上的国内外合伙人、员工都能在这里成长、壮大成为未来的CEO。

他也是一个"屌丝"，上演了一场真正的屌丝逆袭。从农村里走出来的孩子，羞涩，不自信，哑巴英语到国际谈判中的从容、睿智、优雅的转身。

他是一个造梦者，他告诉身边的每一个人，无论你是想做一个业界精英、老板CEO或是哲学家、诗人、乞丐都可以。心有多远，你就能走多远！

他更是一个履梦人，为了实现自己的"中国梦"，先后造访了乌克兰、德国、伊朗、叙利亚、印度尼西亚、智利、澳大利亚、伊拉克、美国、土耳其、厄瓜多尔、尼日利亚、印度、埃及、沙特、巴拿马、玻利维亚等数十个国家。他用他的双脚丈量着世界，也用他的梦想为中国制造与中国创造走向世界贡献自己的力量。

池勇海
Dennis

Born in Xiantao, Hubei Province in 1970, Dennis Chi is of Han nationality and graduated from Wuhan University of Technology with a master's degree in Management Science and from Fudan University with a doctoral degree in Economics.

He is the founder and executive director of a multinational company, devoting himself to building a platform and an organic ecosystem without boundary, which is created, shared and managed by all its members, so that every partner, domestic or foreign, as well as every employee, can grow stronger to become a future CEO.

He used to be a "loser"; however, he performed a real counterattack. Once a shy, unconfident boy from the countryside with extremely poor English speaking proficiency, he has transformed into a business leader who shows calmness, wisdom and grace in international negotiations.

He is a dream-maker who tells everyone around him: "You could be any kind of person, be it professional elite, boss, CEO, or be it philosopher, poet, and beggar— whatever. You can go as far as your heart goes!"

He is also a dream-fulfiller who, in order to realize his "Chinese Dream", has visited dozens of countries: Ukraine, Germany, Iran, Syria, Indonesia, Chile, Australia, Iraq, USA, Turkey, Ecuador, Nigeria, India, Egypt, Saudi Arabia, Panama, Bolivia, etc. He measures the world with his feet, and with his dreams he makes contribution to pushing Chinese manufacture and Chinese creation to the world.

2016 心路历程之感言
Thoughts on the Journey of Heart in 2016

■ Ben Tam

2012 年的因缘，认识了 Dennis 和 Tiger，往后不久又遇上了 Fay。那刻对施璐德公司的印象并不深，因业务交往的两年期间里，只到访过上海办公室一次。心中觉得 Dennis 这位公司领导有点儿独特，但并没有花太多时间去探讨他的独特之处，直觉上他比较诚恳。世事是变动不安的，工作了十年的公司决定撤离香港，且需要通知供应商此信息，我再一次与 Dennis 接触。我本觉得他原是开玩笑的一句："一齐玩吧！"没想到最终真成为施璐德大家庭之一员。回想为什么加入施璐德，仍是那个感觉，他比较诚恳！亦感谢 Dennis 的知遇之情！

隔行如隔山，虽曾操作委内瑞拉石油公司的采购订单，但施璐德的业务范围无

I made the acquaintance of Dennis and Tiger by chance in 2012. Shortly after that, I met Fay. At that time, I did not acquire a deep impression of CNOOD, for I visited its Shanghai office only once during the two years of our commercial contacts. Dennis, as the boss of the company, seemed a little unique to me, but I did not spend more time inquiring into his uniqueness. I had an intuition that he was a man of sincerity. The world kept changing; the company for which I had worked for ten years decided to retreat from Hong Kong. Having to inform all our suppliers, I contacted Dennis again. Dennis said to me, "Why not join us?" Though taking it as a joke, I finally became a part of the big family of CNOOD. When now I look back and ask myself why I chose to join CNOOD, I still get the feeling that Dennis is a man of sincerity. I also owe Dennis a debt of gratitude for his recognition and appreciation.

As the saying goes, "Different trades are separated as by mountains." With the

疑是我的一大挑战。我相信，这缘分的背后，必有它的安排。心中想法虽是如此，但现实上，我还需找到实践的锦囊来支持这信念，否则便成了自我安慰的空想。静下心来，往古圣贤处寻求。仿似是谦卑无心的感应，在众多的书本文章中，让我不经意地止于诸葛亮《诫外甥书》和孔子《论语·子路》。

诸葛亮——《诫外甥书》：

"夫志当存高远，慕先贤，绝情欲，弃疑滞，使庶几之志，揭然有所存，恻然有所感。忍屈伸，去细碎，广咨问，除嫌吝；

experience of carrying out POs form Venezuelan oil firms, the business line of CNOOD was undoubtedly still a big challenge to me. But I believe that there was a God's design behind our encounter. As for the practical business, however, I still need wise counsels to support my belief, which would otherwise be reduced to self-consoling ideas. I calmed down, seeking wisdom from sages of old times. As though an unintentional response to my humbleness, I stopped upon "A Letter of Admonition to His Nephew" by Zhuge Liang and the chapter of "Zilu" in *Analects of Confucius*, even before I noticed it.

It is written in "A Letter of Admonition to His Nephew" by Zhuge Liang that:

A man should keep his noble ambition, admire sages of the past, control his lust and

虽有淹留，何损美趣？何患于不济？若志不强毅，意不慷慨，徒碌碌滞于俗，默默束于情，永窜伏于凡庸，不免于下流矣。"

一个人的志向应当保持高尚远大，仰慕先贤人物，节制情欲，不凝于物，使贤者的志向高高地有所保存，诚恳地有所感受，能屈能伸，抛弃琐碎的东西，广泛地向他人请教、咨询、学习，除去猜疑、狭隘、悭吝，这样即使因受挫折而滞留，又何损于自己美好志趣？何愁理想不能实现？如果意志不坚定，意气不昂扬，徒然随众附和，沉溺于习俗私情，碌碌无为，就将继续伏匿于凡庸之中，终究不免于卑下的地位。

孔子——《论语·子路》："人而无恒，不可以作巫医。"

巫医是古代常以禳祷之术，替人治疗。在当时社会，地位不高，也不受重视。孔子说：人若没有恒心，连巫医也做不了。

感应以相与，圣贤授予的指引是："志"与"恒"。这应是我这个外行初学者与所有新人来到施璐德公司的态度。

在施璐德，体会到公司文化里的一特色，亦是施璐德的管理信念，是鼓励每位员工在工作过程中和个人生活里保持本来的"原始初心"和相互尊重与敬爱如"家人"。相比一直在外资机构任职，公司文化

abandon hesitation, so that the ideals of the virtuous will be cherished and perceived with sincerity. He should be adaptable to circumstances, forsake trivial things, widely seek advice from others, and remove suspicion and narrow-mindedness. By so doing, how can his glorious aspiration be impaired even if he was frustrated with setbacks? Or why should he worry that his ideals might not come true? But if he does not have strong determination and high spirit, and only echoes with what others say, wallows in old customs and personal considerations, without any remarkable results, then he will continue living among inferior people, unable to get rid of his low rank in the society.

In the chapter of "Zilu" in *Analects of Confucius*, it is written that "a man without constancy of purpose cannot be wizard-doctor". The wizard-doctor was a man in ancient times who invoked the gods with sacrifices to cure illnesses for people. In the society, he had a low status and was unappreciated. According to Confucius, a man was incapable of being even a wizard-doctor if he lacks constancy of purpose.

Elements influence and respond to each other, thereby forming a union. "Ambition" and "constancy of purpose" are the guidance given by sages in old times. This is also the right attitude for me as a beginner as well as for all other beginners in CNOOD.

From my experience at CNOOD, I understand that one feature of its corporate culture, also the company's management philosophy, is to encourage all employees to keep "original intentions" both in work

的主导重点在 Company Policy。这一全新概念好像来得有点儿太简单和相对地与一般的公司文化背道而驰。在习以为常的逻辑思维里，有点不合逻辑。因施璐德是一家商业机构，而不是宗教团体，虽然施璐德这个名称，在香港像一所教会的称号。基于格物致知的心态，工作之余，再次尝试寻找答案。

在研究中国古文化过程中，曾参考地球的公转和自转的规律，和其相应产生的变化和引力效应。地球与其他太阳系天体一起环绕太阳运转，太阳是它们共有的中心天体。施璐德推崇的"原始初心"文化，正是以光明与文明为轴心的天地宇宙规律和人类内心渴求的依归。香港富商李嘉诚曾引用宋朝苏东坡一首小词的一句"此心安处是吾乡"来表达他的心境。此一语句出自当时名叫柔奴的歌妓，亦由这一句心的感言，令一代大文豪苏东坡折服和彻底开悟。施璐德公司的核心"由心出发"，柔中带刚，情理交融，细腻柔婉。正是表达

and in private life, while respecting and loving each other like a "family". Before joining CNOOD, I had worked in foreign organizations for a long time, whose corporate cultures emphasized "company policy". This brand-new idea seems somewhat too simple, running in the opposite direction compared to prevalent corporate cultures. It is a little illogical according to logical thinking to which we have been accustomed. After all, CNOOD is a business organization instead of a religious institution, though with a name that sounds more like a church in Hong Kong. With the aim to acquire knowledge by investigation, I tried once again to find the answer in my spare time.

When studying the ancient culture of China, I have referred to the laws of revolution and rotation of the Earth, as well as the corresponding changes and gravitational effect. The Earth and other bodies in the solar system orbit the Sun, which is at their common center. The culture of "original intentions" CNOOD values the most is exactly a reflection of universal laws with light and civilization at the core, and the inner craving of human mind. Li Ka-shing, the Hong Kong business magnate, once quoted a sentence from a short poem written by Su Shi in Song Dynasty— "My home is where my heart is at peace", to express his own state of mind. This famous sentence was originally a remark made by a song girl named Rounu (literally "lithe girl") at that time, and, as an expression of heart, impressed the great writer and brought him to thorough enlightenment. "Start from the

此跨越时空、超越贫富地位、恒久不变的人类内心价值与依归。

"家人"者，《序卦传》曰："伤于外者必反于家。故受之以家人。"《来氏》曰："一家之男女，各尽其职，家道正矣。家正而天下不难定。"《象传》曰："家人之道，修于近小而不妄也。故言必有物而口无择言，行必有恒而身无择行。"

人生是奋斗和前进的过程，遇到挫折伤害之后，必寻求家庭之温暖与安全感。欲治其国者，先齐其家。先从家始，家正则天下化之也。家人是相互包容，相互成就对方的成长，让每位家人在这家庭里，完成个人装备。终能言满天下无口过，行满天下无怨恶。

heart", the core value of CNOOD, blends perfectly firmness and gentleness, feelings and reasoning. Subtle and soft in nature, it expresses the permanent intrinsic human values and principles that are beyond the limitations of time and space, as well as the barriers of being rich and poor.

As for "family", I would like to quote the "Orderly Sequence of the Hexagrams" in *Book of Changes*: "He who is wounded outside will return to his home; hence the hexagram of 'Family' follows." Lai Zhide, a scholar in Ming Dynasty, said: "Men and women of a family fulfill their duties then will the family be in its normal state. Bring family to the normal state, and all under heaven will be established." According to "The Great Symbolism", "The principle of family lies in self-discipline concerning personal matters, getting rid of reckless words and actions. Therefore, the superior man orders his words in accordance with the truth of things so that none of his words is detested by others, while his conduct is uniformly consistent."

Life is a course of endeavor and progress. When we suffer setbacks or injuries, we will automatically seek warmth and security from our families. As the old saying goes, "One who wishes to run his country well must first put his family in order." "The teaching of the saint begins with family; if family is put into proper state, then all men under heaven will be enlightened." Family members embrace each other, and fulfill the growth of each other. Let everyone complete his personal equipment within his family, so that "his remarks may spread to all places under

商业互动，构成商场生意上不断演变的动力。施璐德以管道产品为基础，努力尝试拓展到不同的项目领域。行动与时机是否恰当？相信可能不单是我心中的问题。我也曾尝试从不同的角度去探索。然而，任何改变都可能包含三个基本条件，即"变易""不易"和"简易"。

变易——世界上的事物、人，乃至宇宙万物，没有一样东西不变的。在时，空当中，没有一事，一物，一情况和一思想是不变的，不可能不变，唯一"不变"的是一定要变。穷则变，变则通，通则久。能"长久"才是目标。管道产品的市场变化状况，已不需在此多加注了，现时可能已过了知变而到达识变的阶段。

不易——万事万物随时随地都在变的，可是却有一永远不变的东西存在，就是能变出来万象的那个东西是不变的，那是永恒存在的。在人的领域，万法唯心造。法也者，世间一切的事物。这正是施璐德公司"原始初心，由心出发"的文化与管理轴心。有了此不易的轴心，持续的变化

heaven, yet no error will be found in him; his actions may reach every place under heaven, yet give no cause for complaint."

Business interaction constitutes the source of power for the continuous evolution in the commercial world. Based on pipeline products, CNOOD endeavors to expand into multiple areas of projects. Is it a right action at a right time? This is, I believe, probably a question not only in my mind. I, too, have tried to explore the answer from various aspects. However, any kind of change might comprise three basic prerequisites, namely, change, changelessness, and simplicity.

Change: Among all things in the world, including human beings, and even all beings in the universe, none is without change. In time or space, none of the things, situations or thoughts is without change; it is impossible that they should not change. The only thing that never changes is that there must be a change. It is said in *Book of Changes*, "When a series of change has run all its course, another change ensues, in turn leading to an unimpeded way, which will last long." We aim to "last long". Changing conditions in the market of pipeline products need no further explanation here. Now it is possible that we have passed from the stage of "knowing the changes" to that of "identifying the changes".

Changelessness: All things are changing at any time, in any place. Nevertheless, there is one thing that does not change forever, i.e. the one from which all phenomena derive. It is changeless and exists eternally. As to humans, *dharma* is only fabricated by the mind. By "dharma" we mean all beings in the

才合乎不易的轨道。

简易——宇宙之间的任何事物，有其事必有其理，有这样一件事，就有一定的原理。"有其事而不知其理"，只是人类的智慧不够或经验不足，才找不出它的原理而已。施璐德现时人才济济，拥有众多专门产品、技术和丰富商场经验的贤人。所谓得贤人者得天下，国无不安，名无不荣。天之所助者，顺也。人之所助者，信也。施璐德的公司文化核心取向与其诚信从商的态度，乃恰正是顺乎天而应乎人。

施璐德是什么？

1. 属世之商业平台——从基本生活所需，追求事业理想，发挥个人天赋与所长，实现平生远大志向，以致寻觅缘合的终身伴侣。

2. 共融大家庭——可经历人间至真至诚，互爱互助，宽恕包容。如《系辞下传》："无有师保，如临父母。"使洞达人情与至善，如临见父母之爱与教也。

universe. This is exactly the core of "original intentions" and "start from the heart", the core of CNOOD's corporate culture and management. Only with this changeless core do continuous changes conform to the changeless track.

Simplicity: In the immense universe, where there is a thing, there is a principle. If we do not know the principle of one thing, it is only because we have not yet find it as a result of the inadequacy of our wisdom or experience. CNOOD now boasts a galaxy of talent with expertise in products and technology as well as business experience. As an old saying goes, "A king who gets virtuous and able men can get the world, with a stable country and glorious fame." According to *Book of Changes*, it is said by Confucius:"He whom heaven assists is observant of what is right; he whom men assist is sincere." The core of CNOOD's corporate culture and its honest attitude in doing business are exactly "in keeping with the will of heaven, and in response to the wishes of men".

What is CNOOD?

1. It is a worldly business platform, where you satisfy the basic needs in life, pursue your career goals, bring your natural talent and strong points into full play, achieve your noble ambition, and even find your lifelong companion.

2. It is a big family of communion, the members of which are the most genuine and honest people, who love, help, forgive and embrace each other. Just as is written in "The Great Treatise (Part Two)" of *Book of Changes*,

3. 社会大学堂——工作中实践所学。工余时间，终日乾乾，进德修业。藏器于身，待时而动，何不利之有？

4. 修炼的水月道场——人生虽说是镜花水月。但经过进修、实践、磨炼和印证，终能借假修真，明心见性，达本还原。是无心插柳柳成荫的人生终极价值。

油价低迷，经济不景。令不少企业困难和人心不安定。但这正是孟子所述，让有志之士，能动心忍性，增益其所不能的好机会。《荀子·修身篇》："良农不为水旱不耕，良贾不为折阅不市，士君子不为贫穷怠乎道。"真正商人不因困难而不努力经营，有志者亦不因逆境而不修习。又《庄子·让王篇》："穷亦乐，通亦乐，所乐非穷通也，道德于此，则穷通为寒暑风雨之序矣。"

"though they have neither master nor guardian, but it is as if their parents drew near to them." CNOOD enables you to have a thorough and wise insight into humanity and the supreme good, as if the love and teaching of your parents were always with you.

3. It is a big school that teaches social experience, where you put what you have learned into practice in the daily work. In your spare time, you always keep active and vigilant, advance in virtue, and cultivate all the spheres of your duty. If you act as the superior man in *Book of Changes* does to "keep the weapon concealed with you, and wait for the proper time to move", then how could there be any disadvantages?

4. It is a camp for self-cultivation. Life is but an illusion. However, with the aid of false appearance we can finally seek the truth, understand our mind and nature, and restore the origin through training, practice, discipline and confirmation. This is the ultimate values of life unintentionally fulfilled.

Low oil price and depressed economy has caused much trouble to many companies, disturbing our peace of mind. Nevertheless, it is an excellent chance, according to Mencius, for a man with noble ambition to "stimulate his mind, toughen his nature and increase his capabilities". It is said in the chapter of "On Self-Cultivation" in the book of *Xunzi*, "Just as a good farmer does not fail to plow because of flooding and drought, or a good merchant does not fail to go to the marketplace because of occasional losses on the sale of his goods, so, too, the scholar and gentlemen do not neglect the Way because of poverty and want." That

每一成员是构成施璐德整体之元素，各自本着天行健的态度，常德习教，明以自照，安不忘危，仿如地球自转，产生动力，相应配合其公转引力。寒往则暑来，暑往则寒来，寒暑相推而生生不息。施璐德是难得碰上的机遇，但神而明之，亦全乎其人，自当恐惧修省，戒惧警惕，与一众志同道合的知己好友，共同开拓新的每一天。

本来无一物，何处惹尘埃。

Since all is void from the beginning, where can the dust alight?

is to say, a true merchant does not give up his effort in business because of difficulties, and a man with high ideals does not give up self-cultivation because of adversity. The men endowed with the Way, as said in the chapter of "Declining the Throne" in the book of *Zhuangzi*, "find pleasure in both favorable and unfavorable situations. Their pleasure does not come from visible advantages or disadvantages. With the Way and virtue deeply embedded in mind, they believe that disadvantages would turn to advantages and vice versa, in the way winter would take the place of summer and rain would follow wind."

CNOOD as a whole is made up by all its members, every one of which assumes an unremitting attitude in accordance with the vigorous motion of heaven, maintains constantly the virtue of his heart, and practices the duty of instructions. They illuminate themselves with their own light, without forgetting the danger in times of safety. It is like the rotation of the Earth that produces motive power in concert with the gravity in its revolution round the Sun. When the winter goes, the summer comes; when the summer goes, the winter comes; — it is by this mutual succession of the winter and summer that makes the endless course of life. CNNOD is a rare opportunity for me; however, a true understanding of its profound meaning depends on the right man. I should always keep the fearful feeling and examine myself critically, while maintaining a constant vigilance. I shall work together with my bosom friends who share the common goal to open up every new day in the future.

CNOOD DOCS DEPT.2016 感想
Impressions of CNOOD Documents Department in 2016

■ Angela, Cindy & Tina

在这里，你可以低头看路，也可以仰望星空。

当然，你也可以看看左右，那么多的"美铝帅锅"。

我们这个部门的人，没有什么特别，却又很特别：

坚守实务；

坚守研究；

坚守单证。

不忘初心，着眼当下；

肩负使命，继续追逐和践行梦想。

为自己代言，

我们就是单纯的单证人！

Here, you can lower your head watching the way, or look up at the stars.

You can also, of course, look around you, for there are so many good-looking young persons.

Though having nothing special, people in our department are unique because:

We stick to practice;

We stick to research;

We stick to documents.

We are focused on the present moment, while keeping in mind our initial intentions;

Shouldering our mission, we shall continue seeking and fulfilling our dreams.

We speak for ourselves, as pure documents people.

CNOOD 单证团队，专业、细致、润物无声

The documents team of CNOOD, they are nice and professional.

光阴悠悠自难忘
Long, Unforgettable Times

■ Echo Lee

2012年12月25日晚，久光欢快无限循环的Jingle Bells，在我的记忆中清晰如初。

此后，欢乐圣诞夜就成为施璐德之于我的周年纪念日。

从陌生到熟悉，从熟悉到认同，从认同到同舟共济。

岁月匆匆流过，而我在施璐德的日子却并不那么容易逝去。

我记得每一分收获，每一分感动，每一分执着和每一分期待。

我记得第一次执行订单的忙乱，记得第一次签下PO的欣喜；

记得第一次迈出国门的兴奋，记得第一次拜访客户的紧张；

Fresh and vivid is my memory of the merry and endlessly repeating tune of *Jingle Bells* in Jiuguang Department Store on the evening of December 25, 2012.

Since then, Christmas has become the anniversary between CNOOD and me.

We go from strangeness to familiarity, from familiarity to recognition, and from recognition to shared destiny.

Time elapses quickly, yet my days at CNOOD are not easy to forget.

I remember every time I gained something, every time I was moved, every time I strove persistently, and every time I expected something to happen.

I remember the rush when I handled an order for the first time, as well as the joy when I successfully signed a PO for the first time.

I remember the excitement when I traveled abroad for the first time, as well as the nervousness when I called on a client for the first time.

记得一步步走来师父的谆谆教诲，记得跌倒受伤时安慰我的心灵力量；

记得严寒酷暑并肩奋战的患难情谊，记得欢聚一堂谈笑人生的把酒言欢。

点点滴滴，培养了心智，历练了灵魂。

也使我成为现在的我。

关于未来，有憧憬，有梦想。

明明如月，照亮青春前行的道路。

悠悠光阴，同度人生最美的年华。

愿承载了我们青春和梦想的施璐德，如圣诞夜的乐曲，欢快的无限循环，直到永远。

I remember the earnest instructions from my tutor as I have come all the way along step by step, as well as the power of soul that consoled me when I fell and hurt myself.

I remember the friendship formed during the time when we worked hard shoulder to shoulder in the bitter cold in winter and the extreme heat in summer, as well as the genial chat we had when we got together merrily, drinking wine and talking about life.

Bit by bit, my mind has been enlightened and my soul tempered.

And I have been made the person I am now.

For the future, I still have aspirations and dreams.

They are like a bright moon, lighting up my way ahead.

The time is long, when we are enjoying the best years in life.

May CNOOD, with our youthful dreams, go on like the Christmas melody, merry and endlessly repeating, forever.

李天竹
Echo Lee

李天竹，毕业于复旦大学，围棋职业初段。

This article is written by Li Tianzhu. Graduating from Fudan University, she is a professional Go player of the 1st rank.

桥流水不流
It is the Bridge that Flows, Not the Water

■ Echo Lee

面对不可解的问题，深思的是人类的执着；

面对不可测的奥秘，探索的是人类的好奇；

面对不可知的边界，跨越的是人类的勇气。

我曾经以为自己会下一辈子棋。

在一尺见方的棋盘前，肃杀端坐，看狼烟四起。挥洒纵横，血性豪迈无限。我享受那种征战沙场的感觉。

然而，对胜负的执着，让我最终选择了离开。人生的小舟划向其他不可知的方向。

后来，我过上了曾经以为的别人的人生。如同千千万万普通人一样，做一份普普通通的工作。

职场沉浮，人情冷暖。

Facing insoluble questions, it is the human perseverance that ponders.

Facing unfathomable mysteries, it is the human curiosity that explores.

Facing unknowable boundaries, it is the human courage that leaps.

I once thought I would play the game of *go* for my lifetime.

Sitting straight before the board one *chi* square, solemnly, I could sense the invisible smoke of war rising on all sides. Unstrained, I displayed boundless courage and heroism with great freedom. I enjoyed the feeling of fighting on battlefields.

However, I eventually chose to leave because of my obsession with the results of the game. The small boat of life was steered towards another unknown direction.

Later, I begin to live the life thought to be that of others, doing an ordinary job just like millions of ordinary people.

I experienced ups and downs in workplace, and had a taste of social snobbery.

渐渐明白原来人生并不只有输赢。

很多事情我赢不了,但我也没有输。

甚至输赢本身并不存在。
开始懂得放下争胜的气焰,让自己变得柔软。
渐渐发现只有在放下胜负得失之念时,才能够感到心之所在。

才开始明白棋道原本也是如此。

一日闲来读《易经》,突然想起某本书中曾说,其实世界不只有阴阳两个元素,还有一个常被忽略的第三个元素:限制住阴阳的圆圈。

似有一悟。
那么棋盘,也不止有黑白,尚有棋盘边界为限。
边界之内,有对错。

边界之外,皆虚无。

围棋从数千年前的十路盘,扩大至十三路、十五路,再到今天的十九路。

人类对棋盘上变化的探索一次次打破旧边界。

扩大的边界改变了原来的一切,所有坐标的意义重新定位。

而胜负的游戏依然继续。
人类对求道的执迷也丝毫没有减退。

I gradually understand that life is more than wins and losses.

I cannot win in many things, neither do I lose.

Even the wins and losses do not exist.
I begin to give up the arrogance in competition, becoming softer and more flexible.
I gradually find out that I can feel where my heart is only when I have abandoned the idea of wins and losses.

Until then do I know the Way of *go* is the same from the very beginning.

One day, when I was reading *Book of Changes*, it suddenly struck me that, written somewhere in a book, the world is made up not only by the two elements: *yin* and *yang*. There is a third element that has often been neglected: the circle that confines *yin* and *yang*.

It seemed to have awakened me.
The board of *go*, too, is more than black and white; it has boundaries as its limitations.
There are right and wrong within the boundaries.

Beyond the boundaries, all are void and empty.

The board of *go* with 10 lines appeared thousands of years ago, and evolved to board with 13 lines, 15 lines, and finally the 19 line board today.

Men have repeatedly broken old boundaries in the exploration of changes on the board of *go*.

The expanded boundaries have changed everything, and the meaning of all coordinates are to be redefined.

Yet the game of wins and losses continues.
Men's persistence with the pursuit of the

看着新一代的棋手们愈发深入的局部研究，我觉得他们总有一天又会需要扩大棋盘才能找到新的乐趣。

沉浸在穷尽变化欢乐理想中的年轻棋手们就如同 21 世纪引领人类飞速发展的科学家们，自信地以为自己将征服整个宇宙。

横空出世的 AlphaGo 打乱了棋手们的步伐，也让人类重新开始思考围棋的本质。

我觉得，围棋的本质是不可解。

从某种意义上讲，围棋不是人造的，而是神赐予的。
只是假人之手而已。
因为它包含着人类不可测的深意。
宇宙有着完美智慧。
职业棋手梦中的围棋上帝，即是上帝本人。
围棋，更像是调皮的上帝送给人类的宇宙模型。

透过棋盘，我们看到的是整个宇宙，也看到位于宇宙深处的自己。

棋盘上无法穷尽的变化，正如宇宙中无法解释的谜团。

人类曾经以为科学是无坚不摧的武器，正如棋手至今相信他们无与伦比的战斗力。

如同在棋盘前的探索一般，人类努力

Way has not been weakened in the slightest.

Looking at the increasingly deeper local pattern study of new-generation players, I believe that one day they will need to expand the board again to find new pleasures.

Young players obsessed with the merry ideal of exhausting the changes are just like 21st-century scientists leading human beings to develop rapidly, who are confident that they are going to conquer the whole universe.

AlphaGo, which springing up suddenly, disrupts the paces of human players, and makes human beings to reconsider the essence of *go*.

To me, the essence of the game of *go* is insolubility.

In some sense, the game of *go* was not invented by men, but by God—only by the hands of men—because it has a profound meaning unfathomable to human beings.

The perfect wisdom of the universe.

The god of *go* in the dreams of professional players is God himself.

The game of *go* is more like a model of the universe sent by the mischievous God to human beings.

Through the board of *go*, we can see the whole universe, as well as ourselves in the depth of it.

The inexhaustible changes on the board of *go* is like the mysteries of the universe that cannot be explained.

Men once thought that science was an all-conquering weapon, just as *go* players today believe in their incomparable fighting capacities.

Men are making great efforts to seek the

寻找宇宙的边界。

量子力学的发展和星际旅行分别在微观和宏观层面探索着人类宇宙的边界。

然而，每一次的新发现又引导着我们发现一个更大的边界。

宇宙的边界在哪里，是否真的和围棋盘一样随着人类研究的加深而无限延伸呢？

进入21世纪的人类受困于十九路的棋盘，或许23世纪的人类会在火星上对着二十一路的棋局苦思冥想。

棋盘在，便总有不可解的难题。

人类的自我在，便总有不可消除的痛苦。

可我们依然沉浸于二元对立的世界，因为对立赋予我们意义。

所以棋手的痛苦是上帝的礼物。

所以人类的痛苦是最大的慈悲。

人类文明犹如在沙滩上修建城堡，终有一天会被海浪吞没。

人类的意义不在于城堡，而是存在本身，就如同围棋。

面对不可解的问题，深思的是人类的执着。面对不可测的奥秘，探索的是人类的好奇。面对不可知的边界，跨越的是人类的勇气。

boundaries of the universe, just like their exploration before the board of *go*.

With the development of quantum mechanics and the space flight, men are exploring the boundaries of the universe both microcosmically and macrocosmically.

However, every new discovery leads us to the discovery of larger boundaries.

Where are the boundaries of the universe? Are they expanding infinitely as human study gets deeper, just like the board of *go*?

Human beings in the 23rd century on the Mars might well rack their brains at a 21-line board, just as human beings in the 21st century are trapped by the 19-line board.

There will always be insoluble problems if the board exists.

There will be ineliminable pains if the human ego exists.

But we are still immersed in the world of dualism, for dualism provides us with meaning.

Therefore, a *go* player's pains are the gift from God.

Therefore, men's pains are the greatest mercy.

Human civilization is like a sand castle built on the beach, which would one day be swallowed by the sea waves.

The meaning of human beings does not lie in castles, but in the being itself. Just like the game of *go*.

Facing insoluble questions, it is the human perseverance that ponders. Facing unfathomable mysteries, it is the human curiosity that explores. Facing unknowable boundaries, it is the human courage that leaps.

当棋手面对棋盘时,他面对的是整个宇宙。当人类挑战整个宇宙时,我们面对的是自己的内心。

所以我们仍然愿意沉浸于棋盘中。

泡一杯浓浓的绿茶,看碧水升腾袅袅烟雾。

思绪缓缓探究那不可思量的奥秘。

人从桥上过,桥流水不流。

When a *go* player faces the board, he is facing the whole universe. When a man challenges the whole universe, he is facing his own heart.

Therefore, we are more willing to be lost in the board of *go*.

I make a cup of strong green tea, looking at the smoke curling upward from the green water.

Slowly, mind is delving into the unfathomable mysteries.

When men walk across a bridge, it is the bridge that flows, not the water.

李天竹 / Echo Lee

李天竹,毕业于复旦大学,围棋职业初段。

This article is written by Li Tianzhu. Graduating from Fudan University, she is a professional Go player of the 1st rank.

一次日出
A Sunrise

■ Lilia Chen

天空越来越亮，
离家越来越远。
双脚走得越快，
心却想你越密，
光影落入皱纹，
岁月散出沁香。
最舒适的时候，
竟然那时未觉。
愿
全世界的精彩，
换次你的十年。

The sky is getting brighter and brighter, / and I'm further and further away from home.

The quicker my pace is, / the denser my memory of you becomes.

The shadows fall into the wrinkles, / as times give out fragrance.

I did not notice then/the moment that was the most comfortable.

May I/exchange the wonderfulness of the whole world/ with ten years of yours.

陈理
Lilia Chen

1991年出生，17年学海探索，身心印上了湖湘人的灵气、霸气和匪气，也被传染了卡斯蒂利亚人的阳光与浪漫。
2014年初遇施璐德，一见定"终身"。作为施璐德人，更是拥有了一种情怀：把事情做到极致！

Born in 1991, she experienced seventeen years of academic exploration, on whose body and mind have been stamped the marks of typical people from Hunan Province, i.e. sensibility, aggressiveness and the "gangster-like" manner, while infected with the Castilian sunshine and romance.
She fell in love with CNOOD at first sight in 2014. As a CNOOD member, she cherishes the feelings of doing everything to the utmost.

CNOOD——还原倒立的世界
CNOOD: Restoring the Upside-down World

■ Tina Zhang

您眼中的世界是什么样子？

世界本来是什么样子？
您可曾想过你眼中的世界是倒立的。

可还记得，我们物理课本上学到的，人类眼球的结构是球形的——球形晶体，根据透镜原理，景物投射给视网膜的是上下颠倒的图像，但是大脑自行处理了这个问题，左脑控制右手，右脑控制左手，这样就形成了我们脑海记忆模式的世界成像。但本质上我们眼中的世界是颠倒的。

初接触CNOOD的理念时，对于我这种长期生活在体制内的生物来说是很震撼的，既为之吸引又难免害怕。在这个倒立的世界里，有点惊喜有点意外。

What does the world look like in your eyes?

What does it originally look like?

Has it ever occurred to you that the world in your eyes is upside down?

You might remember what you have learned from the textbook of physics: the human eye is in the shape of a ball, or a spherical crystal; and according to the principle of lens, the image of an object projected on the retina is vertically inverted. Nevertheless, our brain spontaneously solves this problem with its left hemisphere controlling the right hand and the right hemisphere controlling the left hand, thus creating the world imaging mechanism in the memory model of our brain. But essentially the world in our eyes is upside down.

When I got to know CNOOD's philosophy for the first time, it was quite shocking to a person like me, who had been living in the established system for a long time. I was attracted by and afraid of it at the same

它，是反体制反传统的；它，又是正吸引正相合的。

你为看到这样的新世界新系统而兴奋而欢呼，又为它的倒行逆施而疑惑而踌躇。传统的好，还是创新的好，常规的能适应，还是打破常规去突破。

一个新世界排山倒海地扑面而来，你到底是迎向新世界，还是继续沉溺在舒适区？

当听Dennis说，CNOOD要创建一个"少有所养，少有所教，青有所学，壮有所长，老有所依，老有所持"的生态环境时，还是挺疑惑的。青壮年男士是很多公司争抢的香饽饽，而老弱病残妇幼是很多公司想剥离的"不良资产"，就连历时50年的事业单位都要改革养老制度，将这个包袱推向社会了，而CNOOD却要建设一个让所有人都能生长发展效力依靠的生态系统。

当其他企业在强调军事化管理时，

time. In this upside-down world, I felt a little surprised with joy.

It is against the established system and convention; it is of, in the meantime, positive attraction and consistency.

You feel excited and cry out with joy for seeing such a new world and new system, while at the same time filled with doubts and hesitation for its actions that "go against the tide". Which is better: the conventional ways or innovations? Are conventional ways good at adapting to the circumstances? Or shall we break through them?

When a new world is coming in your face with an overwhelming momentum, are you going to embrace it, or continue to stay in the comfort zone?

I was doubtful when Dennis told us that CNOOD was going to create an ecosystem in which "children have the means for their growing up and education, young people have opportunities to learn, people in their prime of life are able to make progress, while the aged have something to depend on and are properly provided for". Young male adults are the favorites that many companies scramble for, while the old, weak, sick, disabled employees, as well as women and children, are "non-performing assets" that a lot of companies want to strip off. Even those 50-year-old public institutions are reforming their pension systems, throwing the burden to the society. Nevertheless, CNOOD is determined to build an ecosystem in which all of us are able to grow, develop, work and have our reliance.

CNOOD pursues liberal growth, while

CNOOD 却实行自由化成长；当很多企业在培养员工成为"螺丝钉"时，CNOOD 却提倡每个人争当 CEO 的思维；当其他企业在强调狼性竞争时，CNOOD 却推行人性互助；当其他企业在试着集权管理时，CNOOD 却搭建公平公正公开的平台；当其他企业要求向上汇报却逐层审批时，CNOOD 提倡的却是快速高效去繁就简、跟随内心；当其他企业在收网套利时，CNOOD 却撒网普惠……

很多企业在选择合作伙伴或者合作企业时，首要的评估条件是"你能为公司带来什么"，而 CNOOD 在选择的时候会评估公司能为你搭建什么样的平台和资源，来帮助你完成一件事。帮人就是帮己。很多企业在薪酬和利益分配时，希望更多的利益留给公司，CNOOD 则着手把利益分给大家，给予的永远多于想要的。

所有的一切都反了方向，而它却是世界本来的模样。

如本文的开头所说，我们脑海里记忆的世界图像本来就是颠倒的，世界有它本来的模样。CNOOD 搭建的生态系统正是按照世界本来的方向，所以才会让人欣喜又向往。也许你已经看世界很久，以为那才是世界的模样，不妨倒立看看真实的世界方向。

other companies lay emphasis on militarized management. It advocates the idea that everyone should have the mindset of CEO, while other companies train their employees to be mere cogs in the machine. It encourages mutual aid with humanity, while other companies emphasize the "wolf" competition. It is building a fair, impartial and open platform, while other companies are experimenting with centralized administration. It advocates the idea of efficiency, simplification and following the heart, while other companies require each employee to report to a senior one at the higher level and wait for approval. It is widely engaged in programs that benefit all, while other companies are beginning to reap profits ...

In selecting cooperative partners, the primary evaluation criterion of many companies is "what can you bring to the company", while CNOOD would ask "what platform and resources can I offer you to help you achieve something". To help others is to help yourself. In the distribution of remuneration and interests, many companies wish to retain more profits while CNOOD aim to hand out the interests to all its members. It always gives more than what it wants to take.

Everything seems in the wrong direction. This is, however, what the world originally looks like.

As is mentioned at the beginning of this article, the world image in the memory of our brain is really upside down, different from what the world originally looks like. The CNOOD ecosystem is built in accordance with the original direction of the world. This is why it makes you joyfully yearn for

也曾疑惑：难道CNOOD要建立一个乌托邦，抑或是实现共产主义理想。其实都不是，中国有句话叫"天生我材必有用"，每个人来到这个世界上都有他的意义和价值，老人有老人的经验、年轻人有年轻人的创新，CNOOD的经营理念和价值体系旨在让人发现自我价值、遵循内心的判断、做最好的自己、100%信任。如果一个人能做到最好的自己，那么还有什么事情是做不好的呢？如果所处的做事平台，有一个100%互信互助的模式，能够减少很多猜忌、解释、协调的消耗，还有什么事情不能做得高效快速极致呢？

it. Maybe you have seen the world for so long a time that you believe this is what it really looks like. If so, you might as well stand upside down to have a look at the real direction of the world.

I once asked:"Is CNOOD going to build a Utopia, or bring the communist ideal into reality?" In fact, neither. There is an old saying in China, "Heaven has made us talents, and we are not made in vain." All men, when they come to this world, have their meanings and values: the old with their experience, and the young with their innovation. The business philosophy and value system of CNOOD aim to enable people to discover their own values, follow the judgment of heart, be the best self, and trust each other a hundred percent. Is there anything that cannot be done successfully if a person can be his/her best self? Is there anything that cannot be done efficiently, speedily and perfectly if the platform for doing business is designed as a model of a-hundred-percent mutual trust and aid, greatly reducing the waste caused by suspicion, explanation and coordination?

公平、公正、公开、共生、共济、共享、开放、开通、开明，是 CNOOD 模式的理念，也正是我们生而为人毕生追求的方向。正是明镜止水以静心，泰山乔岳以立身，青天白日以应事，霁月光风以待人。

也有人怀疑 CNOOD 模式不可能普及，因为人心是复杂的，是有私欲的。那么，不妨想想，千万年来，流传下来的是什么？是真，是善，是美。大道至简，唯善至美，一念成佛，一念成魔，有善念的感化、有真诚的帮助，美好的东西必定流传恒远发扬光大，不好的东西也会消散远离。那么，这样真、善、美的模式，为何不能复制，为何不能普及呢。现在是互联网、物联网时代，所有人都可以通过网络连接世界，所有事物都在朝着公开、透明、共享的方向发展，这是时代的趋势，浩浩汤汤，没有任何力量可以挡住。CNOOD 正是在趋势之前，或引领，或共进，或追赶。

每个人都有自己的梦想，每个人也都有自己想到达的地方，或囿于形势，或囿

Equity, fairness, openness, symbiosis, mutual aid, sharing, open-mindedness, broad-mindedness, and enlightenment: these are the concepts at the core of the CNOOD model, providing the direction that we are born to pursue in our lifetime. We maintain the peace of mind like still water; conduct ourselves in the society with high moral standards; do things with noble character; and treat people openheartedly and frankly.

Some people say that it is impossible to popularize the CNOOD model because of the complexity of human heart with selfish desires. Then just think about the question: What are the things that have been handed down throughout the long history? They are the true, the good and the beautiful. The Great Way is the simplest, and only the good is the most beautiful. One thought in the mind can determine whether you become a Buddha or a devil. With the influence of goodwill and the help with sincerity, good things are sure to be passed down eternally and carried forward, while bad things will disappear. Why, then, can't this model be replicated and popularized? Now is the era of the Internet and IoT (Internet of Things), in which everyone can be connected to the world by networks, and all things are moving toward the direction of openness, transparency and sharing. This is the mighty trend of our times that no power could resist. Sometimes CNOOD leads the trend; sometimes it advances side by side with the trend; sometimes it tries to catch up.

All of us have our dreams, and the destination that we want to reach. But

于现实，或囿于心境，或囿于权衡，最终我们没有到达想去的地方，也放弃了我们曾经的梦想。一生不过百年，有跟随内心能力的不过几十年，是囿于惯性思维的束缚，还是打破那口缸去看一看？

解决难题的办法，有时候就像瓶底的水，当你喝不到够不着的时候，只要倒过来就能喝到了。

不妨来 CNOOD 倒立一下，看看世界本来的模样。

constrained by the situations and reality, or limited by our state of mind or personal calculations, finally we fail to reach the destination and give up the dreams we once had. Life is seldom longer than a hundred years for ordinary people, during which we have no more than several decades when we are able to follow our heart. Shall we be bound by stereotyped thinking, or break the vat to have a look?

Sometimes, the way you solve a problem is like the way you drink the water at the bottom of a bottle: when you cannot reach the water, just turn the bottle upside down.

Why not come to CNOOD and try standing upside down to have a glance at the world as it originally looks like.

张丽萍
Tina Zhang

毕业于华中科技大学机械学院，非典型性工科女，混迹于能源电力行业十多年，在外企国企民企间自由切换。来此一遭，只想多做点事，希望帮助自己帮助他人。爱好广泛，文艺女青年和工程女汉子之间自由转换。

As an atypical female engineer who graduated from Huazhong University of Science and Technology, Tina Zhang has been in the energy and power industry for over a decade, switching without difficulty between foreign companies, state-owned enterprises and private firms. The sole purpose of her life is to do more things, in the hope of helping both herself and others. With a wide range of interests, she transforms freely from an arty young lady to a tough woman engineer and *vice versa*.

塞尔维亚——造梦开始的地方
Serbia, Where We Begin to Create Dreams

■ Tina Zhang

2016 年 3 月，我们第一次通过老朋友 Nemanja 得到塞尔维亚 Brodarevo 1&2 水电站开发权的信息，而很巧的是，我们聘请的土建工程师在 2014 年时已经陪投资方三峡集团的负责人踏勘过该项目。

Brodarevo 1&2 水电站站址位于里姆河上，而里姆河发源于黑山，中下游进入塞尔维亚，开发权属于加拿大 RESERVOIR CAPITAL 公司在塞尔维亚注册的 Renewable Energy Ventures（简称 REV）所有。项目从 2008 年立项开始，耗时 8 年获得了各项证照和完成了可行性研究设计，由于项目设计理念问题，土建工程量和淹没面积增大，导致可行性研究报告的经济分析里投资成本高、财务内部收益率（IRR）低，令在加拿大的母公司失去了投资兴趣，加之，母公司在塞尔维亚的另一个子公司找到了稀有矿种，产生了极大利润，遂从 2013 年起将 Brodarevo 1&2 的开发权进行出售。先后

In March 2016, we first acquired the information about the development right of Brodarevo 1&2 hydroelectric plants in Serbia, through an old friend of us, Nemanja. Coincidently, a civil engineer working for us had made a survey of this project in 2014 with the investors of China Three Gorges Group.

The site of Brodarevo 1&2 hydroelectric plants is on the Lim, a river which rises in Montenegro with its middle and lower reaches flowing through Serbia. The development right was held by Renewable Energy Ventures Ltd (REV), a company registered in Serbia by Reservoir Capital Corp. from Canada. After the initiation of the project in 2008, it took eight years for REV to complete all the permitting and feasibility study of the project. But its Canadian parent company was no longer interested in the project because of the high investment costs and low internal return rate (IRR) reflected in financial analysis in the feasibility report,

有多家欧洲和中国的能源投资公司赴塞尔维亚REV进行磋谈和踏勘，价格也从当初的叫价700万欧元降到500欧元最后到300欧元，均由于投资收益率不好、购买关系复杂而放弃。

2016年6月12日，CNOOD、CEEC以及HRC的工程师组队前去塞尔维亚考

as a result of increased workload of civil engineering and flooded area due to design concept. In addition, another Serbian subsidiary of Reservoir Capital found rare mineral resources, which produced substantial profit. In 2013, Reservoir Capital decided to sell off the development right of Brodarevo 1&2. Several European and Chinese energy investment companies went to Serbia to negotiate with REV and make on-the-spot surveys, with the asking price from the initial seven million euro to five million and again three million euro, but all were abandoned because of low rate of return on investment (ROI) and complicated relationships.

On June 12, 2016, engineers from CNOOD, CEEC and HRC went together to

察 Brodarevo 1&2，和业主 REV 公司进行了会谈，此时业主要价仍然是 700 万欧元。我们同时接洽了当地律师，并请律师对 REV 做了详尽调查。调查显示 REV 公司存在欠发薪水、拖欠律师费、站址土地购买不全、证照过期等问题，涉及金额约 130 万欧元。

鉴于上述种种问题，我们改变了购买 REV 的思路，准备在塞尔维亚注册新公司，申请 Brodarevo 1&2 河段的开发权，但是需时至少 2 年。经与 Nemanja 和老马商量，这个方案太慢。此间，也多次与 CEEC 协商推进办法，均以项目收益率低，集团上层不能通过的理由没能进行下去。向外求不成，只能向内求，经过尼泊尔项目的尝试，我们找到了另外一种工作模式，对于投资额不大（小于 5 000 万美元）的项目，采用 30% 的资本金和 70% 的银行贷款模式。遵循这种模式，Nemanja 很快在塞尔维亚找到两家银行有兴趣贷款给投资能源电站的投资人。

2016 年 12 月 25 日凌晨，在万家团圆的圣诞夜，我们得到了最好的圣诞礼物，Dennis、林旭新（可行性研究设计工程师）、丁红梅（书院设计工程师）以及我

Serbia for an investigation of Brodarevo 1&2. They had meetings with REV, the owner of the project, whose asking price was still seven million euro. We consulted a local lawyer who was requested to conduct the due diligence on REV. The results indicated existing problems including wage arrears, delayed payment of lawyer's fee, incomplete purchasing of the site land and expiration of permitting etc, which involved an amount of approximately 1.3 million euro.

Because of these problems, we changed the idea about the acquisition of REV, planning to register a new company in Serbia to apply for the development right of Brodarevo 1&2 section of the river. The procedure would take at least two years. After talking with Nemanja and Lao Ma, we thought it was too slow. We also discussed the way of pushing it with CEEC several times, but the attempt failed for reasons of low rate of return and the disapproval from the senior management of CEEC. We had to seek solutions by ourselves since we could not find external help. In fact, we had found another way after the Nepali project: for any project with an investment less than fifty million dollars, we could adopt an approach combining 30% of capital and 70% of bank loans. Following this approach, Nemanja soon found two banks in Serbia who were interested to make loans to energy power plant investors.

On the dawn of December 25, 2016, the Christmas Eve for family reunion, we received the best gift: Dennis, Lin Xuxin (engineer for feasibility study design), Ding Hongmei

再次飞往塞尔维亚。兵分两路，Dennis 和 Tina 负责与 REV 公司以及银行的洽谈，林旭新和丁红梅负责现场站址的复勘和重新规划。

REV 公司已经有近一年没有给员工发薪水，所以员工们看着我们如此诚意地去购买这个公司，呈现出明显的积极气象，和 6 月份死气沉沉的样子完全不一样。

一方面，在与 Erste Bank（奥地利）和 UNI Credit Bank（意大利）两家银行洽谈后，两家都表示出极大的兴趣，也表示可以考虑联合贷款降低风险的方式。另一方面，REV 公司也急于知道我们的购买价格，Peter 还亲自约饭表达自己加入的意愿以及自己团队的待遇要求，然后就是眼巴巴地询问购买价格。此时，万事俱备，只欠价格，其实所有人应该都在等待这个价格。清晨我和 Dennis 碰面的时候，他提出 50 万欧元的想法，通过 Peter 私人 50 万欧元购买，然后加价 20 万欧元从 Peter 手上转购。晚饭时，Peter 和老马多次询问购买价格，所有人都望眼欲穿，本以为 Dennis 会在 Peter 面前报出这个价格，出乎意料，Dennis 一直将价格藏在肚子里，漠视大家期待的眼神，那天的晚饭大家都在疑问和困惑中散去。

(engineer for academy design) and Tina Zhang flew to Serbia again. We were then divided into two groups: Dennis and Tina were going to negotiate with REV and the banks, while Lin and Ding were in charge of a re-survey and re-planning of the site.

REV hadn't paid salaries to its employees for almost one year. When they saw our sincere effort in the acquisition, there was obviously a positive atmosphere, totally different from the spiritless mood in June.

After the meetings with Erste Bank (Austria) and UNI Credit Bank (Italy), both of them showed great interest and expressed their consideration of a joint loan to lower risks. On the other hand, REV was eager to know our bidding price. Peter even invited us to dinner, at which he expressed his wish to join and the salary expectation of his team, and then anxiously inquired about our bidding price. At that moment, everything was ready; all we need was the price. As a matter of fact, all of us were waiting for it. When we met Dennis early in the morning, he suggested a plan in which Peter was going to acquire the company personally at the price of five hundred thousand euro and then transfer it to us with a markup of two hundred thousand euro. At the dinner, Peter and Lao Ma inquired about the price many times, while everyone was looking forward to hearing it with eager expectation. We thought Dennis would announce his price in Peter's presence; but he didn't. He just managed not to disclose it, ignoring our expectant eyes. The dinner ended; everyone was filled with doubts and confusion.

Dennis 到底在想什么，他要什么时候报出价格，他要报价多少，每个人都在心里打鼓。

原来，Dennis 意在要汇合踏勘的人详细了解这条流域后的情况以及第一个开建项目的可行性。

得到踏勘工程师肯定的意见后，第二日，我们集齐人马，浩浩荡荡地开往 REV 公司了。在听取了我们的 5 级电站规划（每一级约 15 MW）后以及建设的规划后，REV 公司的女老板很是佩服，一副英雄相见恨晚的样子。也许她也曾在里姆河上有一番抱负，奈何时也运也，她的设计规划没有成功，空耗 8 年青春，都付诸东水。

谈到价格时，我们以为见证奇迹的时刻到了，商场硝烟四起，唇枪舌剑、你来我往，所有我们能想到的景象都没有呈现，Dennis 和女老板被关到小黑屋去谈价格了，千斤处是绵柔力，一切硝烟在无形。不过半小时，在 Dennis 出来后，我们眼巴巴地看着他的时候，没有下文，没有铺垫，他竟带着我们和 REV 的成员握手说再见了。

难道谈得不好，到底出价多少，他们谈了什么，对方什么要求，十万个为什么

What on earth our boss was thinking? When would he announce his price and how much? We all felt uncertain.

It turned out, however, that Dennis was waiting for people in charge of the survey to get more detailed information of the river basin and the feasibility of the first project to be started.

Receiving positive opinions from the engineer who had finished the survey, all of us went on the way to REV the next day. The lady boss of REV was deeply impressed and regretted not having met us earlier, when she had listened to our design for a five-cascade hydroelectric plant (approximately 12 MW each cascade) and the plan for construction. She probably had her ambition on the Lim years ago, too, but her design and plan did not help her to fulfill the ambition. Eight years of her youth was lost in vain, forever gone with the flowing water of Lim.

When it came to the part of price, we thought it was time to witness a miracle: all the heated arguing and quarreling on the negotiating table. But none of the scenes we could imagine ever appeared. Dennis and the boss of REV went into a small dark room to negotiate over the price. Facing the extremely heavy pressure, he displayed the strength of softness. All the smoke of gunpowder was invisible to us. Barely half an hour later, we eagerly looked at Dennis as he came out of the room. But without saying additional words, he led us to shake hands with REV people and bade them farewell.

Millions of questions were going round in our heads: Was the negotiation unsuccessful?

在我们脑子里打转。

"我出价 30 万欧元!"

30 万欧元?我们实在不敢相信,REV 公司 8 年的努力、1 000 多万欧元的投入,Dennis 竟出价 30 万欧元,我真想问是谁给他的勇气,我真担心会被别人打出去。

然而,Dennis 就是 Dennis,他只根据实际价值和实际可操作性去做事,对方的确花了很多时间和金钱在这个项目上,但是一开始设计的思路错了,走得越远,损失越大,可是这个损失不是我们造成的,对我们今后也没有帮助,它目前的价值就是 100 万欧元内。

Dennis 表明,如果 REV 同意 30 万的价格,第二日立即签订合约,立即进行购买程序。第二日,REV 通过老马传话,希望以 60 万欧元出卖,但是我们仍然坚持 30 万的价格。

截至发稿,双方还在胶着和心理战,但是,我们的行动已经开始。

也许,塞尔维亚将是我们最开始进行能源投资的地方,是我们进行全球互联网电力的一个开端,是我们造梦最开始的地方,是我们创造从无到有的自然机会。我们一个电站一个电站的去建设,为暂时黑

What was the bidding price? What did you talk about? What did REV demand?

"I offered three hundred thousand euro."

Three hundred thousand euro? We could hardly believe that Dennis should offer such a price for a project in which eight years and more than ten million euro had been put. I really wanted to ask him from where he gathered his courage. I was even afraid of being driven out.

This was exactly how Dennis did things: always and only in accordance with the real value and the practicality of a project. It was true that REV had spent a huge amount of time and money on the project, but they were wrong in the design from the very beginning;—the further they went, the bigger the loss was. But the loss was not caused by us, and was of no help to us in the future. Therefore, the project was worth less than one million euro at that time.

Dennis stated that we would sign the MOU and start the procedure the next day if REV agreed to the price of three hundred thousand euro. The next day, REV sent us a message through Lao Ma that they would sell off the project at six hundred thousand euro. But we insisted on the price of three hundred thousand euro.

The two sides remained at a stalemate in their psychological warfare when I finished this article. But our action had begun.

Maybe Serbia will be the place where we make our first investment on energies, where we initiate the global electricity network, and where we begin to create dreams. It offers us a natural opportunity

暗落后的地方输送光明，我们一条流域一条流域的去开发，打包放进能源公司上市，让全球的人民都享受电力带来的红利；我们一个区域一个区域的去连通，区域电网联动全球电网，最终实现全球电力互联，让全球的人民都享受到电力带来的发展。未来，技术在发展、能源在融合、观念在革新、全球在联通，互联网电力只是一个开始，将来必然是能源电力互联、动力自然相通，最终万物与自然融通，机器生物化，生物工程化，还原一个一体的世界，万宗归一。这是一项没有边界的事业，这是一个没有尽头的梦想。我们用今生去造梦，前仆后继、勇往直前。梦想没有尽头，生命便没有尽头。

愿我们CNOODers都是造梦者，在未来砥砺前行。我们记住今天，并为此时此刻的梦想去努力，将来有一天，我们会感谢这一刻的开始，感激这一刻的自己和身边的伙伴。

of creating something from nothing. We will begin our construction, one power plant after another, sending light to the temporarily dark, less developed regions; we will initiate our development plan, one river basin after another, packing them into a listed energy company and allowing people all over the world to benefit from electricity; we will make our effort to connect, one region after another, all local power grids to the global grid, finally creating a global electric network and extending the fruits of electric development to all people on the earth. With the progress of technology, the integration of energies, the renewal of ideas and the connectivity throughout the world, the global electricity network is but a beginning. We will live in a world in which electricity and other powers are naturally interconnected, and eventually all things are integrated with nature. Machines will become biological, while biological resources are exploited by engineering methods. This will be a world restored to unity; while all elements are directed toward one destination. This is a cause without boundary, and a dream without end. We spend our lifetime to create dreams, bravely advancing one after another. There is no end to life, as there is no end to dreams.

We wish all CNOODers are dream-creators, moving forward through hardships. We will remember this day, and make effort for the dreams of this very moment. One day in the future we shall be grateful to the beginning at this moment, and to ourselves as well as the companions beside us.

张丽萍
Tina Zhang

毕业于华中科技大学机械学院，非典型性工科女，混迹于能源电力行业十多年，在外企国企民企间自由切换。来此一遭，只想多做点事，希望帮助自己帮助他人。爱好广泛，文艺女青年和工程女汉子之间自由转换。

As an atypical female engineer who graduated from Huazhong University of Science and Technology, Tina Zhang has been in the energy and power industry for over a decade, switching without difficulty between foreign companies, state-owned enterprises and private firms. The sole purpose of her life is to do more things, in the hope of helping both herself and others. With a wide range of interests, she transforms freely from an arty young lady to a tough woman engineer and *vice versa*.

患难之交见真情

成功就是跌倒九次、站起十回

A friend in need is a friend indeed!
Success is falling nine times and getting up ten

■ Wael Ismail

亲爱的朋友们：

很高兴认识到我们都是施璐德大家庭的一员。在本文的开头，我想先讲一个关于友谊的小故事。故事说的是：有两个好朋友一同行走在树林中。

有一次，他俩起了争执，其中一人扇了另一人耳光。

被扇耳光的那人很痛，但没说什么，只是在沙上写下："今天，我最好的朋友扇了我耳光。"

二人继续前行，发现有一座湖，他们就下去游泳。先前被扇耳光的那人险些溺水，幸好被他的朋友救起。

这人上岸后，在石头上写下："今天，我最好的朋友救了我的命。"

那个扇他耳光、后来又救了他的朋友，问他："当我伤到你的时候，你写在沙上；现在你却写在石头上。这是为什么呢？"

他回答道："有人伤害我们时，我们应该记在沙上，风会把它擦去。但是，有人做了好事，我们应该铭刻在石头上，无

Dear friends,

Happy to understand that we are part of big and good family Cnood. I would like to start my article from small parable: The parable of friendship which tells the story of two friends walking in the woods.

Once they had an argument and one of them slapped another.

Feeling pain, but without saying anything wrote on the sand:"Today my best friend slapped me".

They continued walking and found a lake where they went swimming. The one that got slapped nearly drowned, and his friend saved him.

When he came to shore, he wrote on a stone:"Today my best friend saved my life."

The one who slapped him and who saved his life asked him: When I hurt you, you wrote in sand and now you write on stone. Why?

Friend replied: "When someone hurts us we should write it on sand, so the winds would erase it. But when someone does

论怎样刮风都不会被擦去。"

我希望，在我们施璐德这个大家庭，这本书就像故事中的石头那样，可以让我们在上面书写共同经历的精彩回忆。

2014年以来，我与大家齐心奋战，共渡难关，成果颇丰，这一切都要归功于富有凝聚力的团队协作。

我们是一个强有力的团队，每天都在成长，每天变得更强；我们秉持共同的价值观与愿景，直面困难，解决困难，直到实现我们的目标。

只要我们在一起，就一定强大无比！
此致

something good, we should engrave it on stone so no wind would erase it."

Within our Cnood family, I hope this book will be something as a stones where we can write all good and successful stories which we pass through together.

Since 2014 we have been working hard together, shared difficult moments and achieved some good results, but all thanks to the cohesive work.

As a strong team together, we grow stronger every day sharing common values and vision, facing difficulties and dealing with them to reach our goals.

TOGETHER WE ARE STRONG!
Best Regards,

Wael Ismail

CNOOD 海外合伙人。
Oversea partner of CNOOD.

亚沙·感悟——一路有你

You Are Always with Us: Reflection on the "Asian-Pacific Business Schools Desert Challenge"

Dennis

第一日

时间安排，迟到，别人嫌弃。内松外紧，对自己要求严格。

要有眼界，宽阔的眼界，要有心里的旗帜，才永不迷路。

放弃的，并不是不行，而是他们心里放弃了。

新人要敢于面对挑战，做最优秀的自己，您行的。

新人会成熟，要给予新人更多机会。开放的心态，互相包容、互相成就和互相成全的心态，会给他们一个更加美好的未来，会给CNOOD一个更加美好的未来。

【Dennis】

The First Day

You will be disliked by others if you are late due to bad scheduling. Be loose inside and tight outside, and be strict with yourself.

Have a vision, a broad vision. Have a banner in your heart so you will never lose your way.

Some people give up, not because they are incapable, but because they have given up in their heart.

New members should bravely face challenges and be the best self. You can make it.

New members will grow up. They ought to be given more opportunities. With the open-mindedness and the mentality of forgiving each other, fulfilling each other and helping each other to achieve their goals, there will be a better future for them as well as for CNOOD.

第二天
永不言弃,做团队的核心骨。

我们每个人都有自己的纠结,解决它,就是您生命中的丰碑;放弃他,会成为您人生中无法逾越的障碍,直到您解决他。

事情不像我们想象的简单,但也不会像我们想象的复杂。去做,再复杂的也会简单;不做,再简单的事情也会复杂。

跟对人,学会判断方向;跟错人,学会判断方向;自由而无用的灵魂。

"我们是名校过来的,怎么这种待遇。"复旦-港大 MBA 女生语。自己是什么人,就会有什么待遇;头天浪费。

The Second Day

Never give up. Be the backbone of the team.

All of us have knotty problems. If you solve it, it will be a monument in your life; if you give it up, it will become an insurmountable obstacle in your life until you have solved it.

Things are not as simple as we imagined, nor are they as complicated as we imagined. If we set about to do one thing, no matter how complicated it is, it will become simple; if we don't do it, no matter how simple it is, it will become complicated.

If you are with the right person, learn to judge the direction; if you are with the wrong person, learn to judge the direction; free and useless souls …

"We're from famous colleges. How could we be treated like this?" —A remark by a female Fudan University-HKU MBA candidate. You will be treated according to the kind of person you are. The first day is wasted.

第三天

在沙漠里，每个人都认为自己的路是最短的，但几乎都在走弯路。

中国人民大学的组织非常好，有的人准备得不好。

天气非常好，大雨雷电之后，空气清新润湿。

处处都是旺盛的生命力。

奖牌，是一种经历，是自己对自己的认可。没有完成的，不领奖牌。

The Third Day

When in the desert, everyone believes that the path he/she takes is the shortest; however, almost all of them are taking a roundabout route.

The team from Renmin University of China does a good job in organizing, while some are not well prepared.

The weather is excellent. After the heavy rain and thunders, the air is fresh and humid.

There is exuberant vitality here and there.

The medal represents an experience, and a self-recognition. Those who have not finished the course do not receive one.

Andy

有些事情，不要想自己可不可以做到，只要你想做了，认真去准备吧，你会发现事情没有你想象的那么难；

速度没有方向重要，方向没有心态重要；不要纠结于选了"错误"的方向，只要你不忘初心，每条路都是正确的道路。

简单的事情，只要做多了，也可以找到省力的方法。比如走什么样的路省力，怎么走路最省力。

不要畏惧困难，你看到的高坡不一定难走，你选择的平地也不一定简单。

【Andy】

As for some things, stop hesitating whether you can do it or not. Just go and seriously prepare to do it once you want to. You will find that they are not as difficult as you imagined.

The speed is less important than the direction, and the direction is less important than mentality. Don't be upset about the "wrong" direction you have chosen. Every way is the right way if you keep in mind the original intentions.

Even for simple things, when you have repeated them many times, you can find an easier way of doing them, for example the path that saves your effort.

Don't be afraid of difficulties. The high slopes you see are not necessarily hard to climb, while the flat grounds you have chosen are not necessarily easy to walk on.

要有一个大的目标，并把大的目标分解成一个个小的目标，那样会轻松很多。

心要保持年轻，那才是青春。

Fay

强大的精神与健康的身体，太重要！没有强大的精神，身体容易放弃原有能力完成的事情；没有健康的体魄，精神也会很艰辛！

凡事要有自己的节奏！跟随潮流或者能者，对自己也许太快，也许太慢，但无法长久地生活与工作。一定要走准自己的节奏，才能轻松前行并且享受沿途！

不停歇，持续前行、积累，跑步如此、学习如此，只要在路上、在积累就一定会有收获，距离目标越来越近！

终点，大多数人都有能力到达，但也许最后会发现终点不是目标。享受过程也相当重要！

出于本能，适应潜能一直在。相信自己！

每个人，都有各自的背负。靠自己，不给他人增加负担。路要自己走，自己的人生只能自己完成！

结局既定。以更包容的心态，找回自己走进腾格里的初衷，感恩一起走过的三天。

Have a big goal, and break it down into smaller goals. That will be much easier.

Keep young in your heart;—that is youth.

【Fay】

It is so important to have a strong mind and a healthy body. Without a strong mind, the body is likely to give up what it ought to be able to complete; without a healthy body, the mind will undergo many hardships.

Have your own rhythm in doing everything. It will be too fast or too slow for you if you only follow the trends or the able ones; in that case, you cannot have your life or work for long. Only by keeping precisely your own rhythm can you move forward easily while enjoying the journey.

Never stop. Keep moving on. Accumulate. It is true with running as with learning. As long as you are on the way and keep accumulating, you will achieve something and get closer to your objective.

Most people have the ability to reach the goal, but maybe finally they will find that the goal is not what they originally aimed for. It is equally important to enjoy the process itself.

Out of our instinct, the potentiality of adaptation always exists. Believe yourself.

Everyone has his own burdens. Depend on yourself; do not add burdens to others. You have to walk your own way; no one can finish your journey of life except yourself.

The die is cast. Find back your original intentions of entering the Tengger Desert with a more forgiving mind, and be grateful to the three days that we walked together.

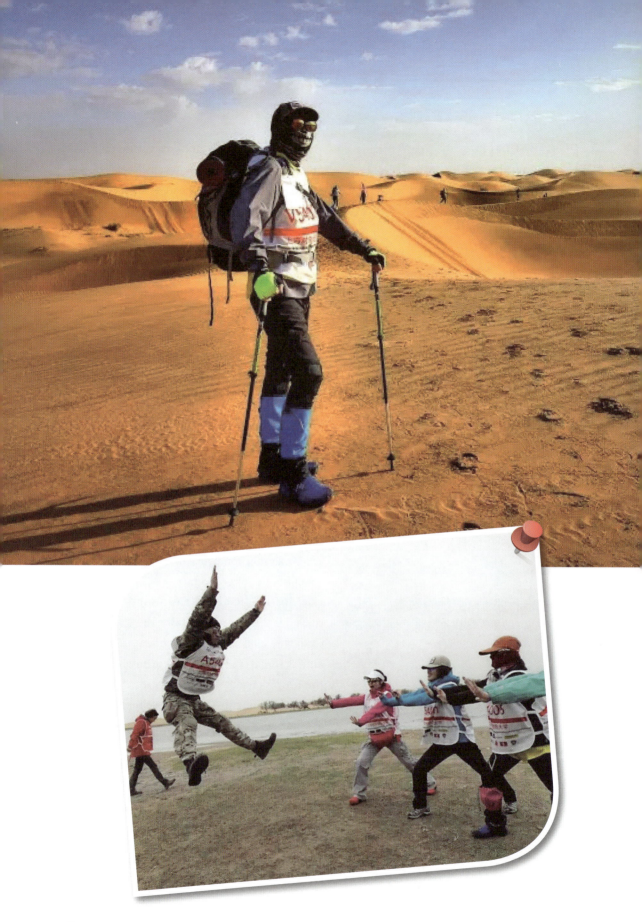

Connor

不是每个人都有机会远离城市，逃离原本喧闹的生活。

亚沙教会我淡定从容。

有些路，需要一个人走，哪怕安静得你不知道前行的目标。

有时会觉得沙坡很高，爬坡很累，总想着怎么找到最平坦的路，来节省体能。

但亚沙最为享受的也就是上坡的难于上青天，和下坡的酣畅淋漓。

想来人生亦如此，用平淡的心，去走坎坷的路。

【Connor】

Not everyone has the chance to be far away from the city, escaping from the bustling life.

The Desert Challenge teaches me to calm down with self-possession.

Even if you have to walk alone some part of the way, or it is too quiet that you do not know where the objective is.

The dunes seem too high for you, and the climbing is exhausting; what you hope the most is to find the flattest route to save physical strength.

However, the most enjoyable part of the Desert Challenge is the extremely hard way when going up the slope, and the absolute freedom when going down.

Life, it occurs to me, is like this too. I will go on the rough road with a plain heart.

特别的爱给父亲
Special Love to My Father

■ Tong Ming

一直想写点什么给父亲。

人说父子之间的感情很微妙，原因是两个独立个性的男人都想证明只有自己才是最刚强的。这话不假。作为家中的长子，长到24岁，我从没面对面地对父亲表达过一句想念、爱意的话。但说心里话，对父亲的爱在心底却与日俱增。

父亲是教师，在数百里外的家乡中学教外语。听奶奶讲，父亲从小生性要强，要做的事一定是最好的。父亲平时对学生要求很严格。父亲教过的班级统考时总是名列前茅。学校里父亲不是资格很老，但在100多位教师中却很有威信。父亲生性倔强，认准的事便不能改。父亲不认为当教师吃亏，在如今"下海"已成为越来越多的人的一种神往时，父亲痴心如故，仍一如昔日拿着粉笔站在讲台前。在这一点上，我继承了父亲固执的个性，父亲在我心里的形象越来越高大。

I have been always thinking about writing something for my father.

The feelings between father and son, it is said, are delicate, because either of them, with independent character, wants to prove that he is the strongest. It is true. As the eldest son in the family, I have never said any words of missing or affection to my father face to face. In the bottom of my heart, however, the love to my father is growing with every passing day.

My father is a teacher. He teaches foreign language in a local middle school hundreds of miles away from home. According to my grandmother, he has been eager to outdo others ever since childhood and has always aimed to be the best in whatever he has chosen to do. He is strict with his students. All the classes he has taught come out among the best in the general examinations. He does not have advantage in seniority, but still enjoys high prestige among more than one hundred teachers of the school. He is of

去年教师节，正值《锦西日报》举办"浪漫夏日"诗歌大奖赛，一直想写点什么给父亲的愿望终于实现了。我的一首写给父亲、写给教师节的《画一轮太阳给父亲》发表在9月12日的《锦西日报》上，被评为二等奖。我认真地把它剪下来，寄给远在数百里外家乡的父亲。在把信投进邮筒的那一刻，我想象着父亲见到信的情景，这是儿子第一次给父亲爱的礼物，我难以抑制内心的激动。

大学毕业，在经历了种种放弃之后，我到了辽西海滨小城。谋生在另一片天地里相处在新一丛人群中。日子一天天过去，但每每午夜梦回，心灵深处最最依恋的仍是那份难舍的亲情，最最热望的仍是父母的牵挂。难得一次回到家里，父母脸上便绽满了笑意，逢人便说儿子回来了，晚上便总要和父亲长谈直到深夜母亲催促说"该睡了，你们爷儿俩。"回来的时候，每次透过车窗，都能看到父亲的身影一直挥手站在路旁……

a stubborn disposition; what he has set his mind on cannot be changed. He does not think it is a loss to be a teacher. When doing business is becoming the admiration of more and more people nowadays, he is infatuated with his work as before, holding the chalk and standing in front of the podium. I has inherited this obstinacy of my father, and his image becomes bigger and bigger in my mind.

On the Teacher's Day of last year, my wish of writing something for my father was finally realized when a poetry contest named "The Romantic Summer Days" was held by *Jinxi Daily*. "Drawing a Sun for Father", a poem written by me for my father and for Teacher's Day was published in the September 12th issue of *Jinxi Daily* and was awarded a Second Prize. I carefully clipped it off from the newspaper and sent it by mail to my father, who was in hometown hundreds of miles away. When I put the letter into the postbox, I could imagine the scene of my father receiving and reading it. This is the first time the son gave his father a gift of love. I could hardly restrain the excitement in my heart.

Graduating from college, I came to the little coastal city in the west of Liaoning Province after several times of giving up. I have been trying to earn a living in a different world with a new group of people. Time goes by; but often when I wake up from a dream at midnight, I feel that the unbreakable family bond is still the deepest attachment in the bottom of my heart, and that my parents' solicitude for me is still what I am longing for most ardently. Every time I get a chance to go

父亲来信了，说母亲身体很好，妹妹学习用功，叮嘱我离家在外，学会照顾自己，踏实工作，老实做人——当然都是老师教导学生的话。父亲提到那首诗他看过了，没有评价，但在信结尾的地方，父亲第一次写上了"我爱你儿子。"

back home, my parents will be all smiles and tell everyone that their son is back. At night, I always have long chats with my father until my mother urges us, "It's time to sleep, both of you." When I am leaving home, I can see through the window the silhouette of father, standing on the roadside and waving his hand.

In his reply, my father said that my mother was very well and my little sister studied hard. He urged me, who was away from home, to learn to take care of myself and, while being earnest and down-to-earth, to be an honest person—all are a teacher's usual instructions to his students, of course. He also mentioned that he had read my poem, but without comment. However, at the end of the letter, he wrote for the first time the following words: "I love you, my son."

佟明
Tong Ming

施璐德合伙人，清华大学 MBA 硕士，鞍山作家协会成员。其既有脚踏实地的企业家精神，又有星空与远方诗人的情怀。

Tong Ming is a partner of CNOOD ASIA LIMITED. He received an MBA degree from Tsinghua University. He is also a member of Anshan Writers Association. He is a man with the down-to-earth entrepreneurship, as well as the poetic feelings of the "starry sky and remote land".

施璐德集团公司年鉴
CNOOD 2017 To 2016

■ 施璐德财务部
CNOOD Accounting Department

公司名称：施璐德亚洲有限公司
公司注册地：
成立时间：2008 年 9 月 18 日
创始人：池勇海博士

时间推着人类前行，但历史必将被铭记。

从无到有从来就是一个难题，遑论建立一个公司。以史为鉴可以知兴替，在度过初时的艰难困苦之后回望，未来的每一步路才会走的更加坚定。

一、大事记

2008 年

2008 年，在全球摧枯拉朽般的金融危机的惨烈背景下，施璐德亚洲有限公司在中华人民共和国香港特别行政区悄然诞生。从此全球 EPC 业界多了一个响亮的名字——施璐德。

Company Name: CNOOD ASIA LIMITED
Registered Address:
Time of Incorporation: September 18, 2008
Founder: Dr. Dennis Chi

Time pushes men forward, while history is to be remembered.

It has always been hard to create something out of nothing; to start a company from scratch, needless to say, is even harder. Draw lessons from history, and you will learn the causes of rise and fall. Reviewing the past after going through initial difficulties and hardships, we are sure that every step in the future will be firmer.

1. Chronicle of Events

2008

In 2008, CNOOD ASIA LIMITED was quietly born in Hong Kong Special Administrative Region, People's Republic of China, against the tragic background of the global financial crisis sweeping across the world.

上海代表处办地址：上海静安区万航渡路1号环球世界大厦B705室。

宁波结算中心随之成立，办公地址：费凤家书房。

2009年

2009年1月施璐德第一次年会在宁波召开，与会人员三人：费凤、池勇海、张召环。年会以聚餐的形式进行，围于一桌，两荤一素外加一瓶老酒。形式简单，没有豪言壮语，只有对未来的憧憬。

From then on, there has been a new, preeminent name in the EPC industry–CNOOD.

Shanghai Office Address: Rm705, Unit B, Universal Mansion, No. 1 Wanhangdu Road, Jing'an District, Shanghai, China

Shortly afterwards Ningbo Settlement Center was set up with the following office address: a study at Feifeng's home.

2009

In January 2009, CNOOD's first annual meeting was held in Ningbo with three participants: Feifeng, Dennis Chi, and Zhang Zhaohuan. We dined together for the meeting: sitting around the table, with two meat dishes and one vegetable dish, plus a bottle of wine. It was simple in form with no brave words, except the vision about the future.

2009 年 7 月，第一个业务合同签订，客户 SALIZIGITTA 合同金额 29 029.68 美元，合同于 8 月圆满完成，公司在从此在全球业务中迈出了最为关键的坚实的一步。

2009 年 12 月 30 日香港施璐德亚洲有限公司上海代表处正式成立，公司从此形成了以香港为基地，上海为业务中心，宁波为结算中心的新局面，从此，公司翻开了快速成长的一页。

2010 年

经过 Dennis 一年多的辛勤工作，随着人员配置到位，公司业务开始步入正轨。公司相继成为 CUNADO、MAYA ENTERPRISES、CORRTECH TRENCHLESS、HAFFARI 的供应商，完成销售额 7 亿美元。合同 CN2010007010（即：Po.504/8524）遭到 Salzgitter 退货 347 吨，并向我公司提出索赔。

2011 年

2011 年，CUNADO 成为公司的主要客户；公司成为 ARCELORMITTAL 的供应商，业务有了新的突破。

2011 年公司以每股 1 港元的价格共发行股份 1 000 万股，上海办公室从 B705 搬迁到 B1001，办公场所扩大。

In July 2009, CNOOD signed its first ever business contract, the client being SALIZIGITTA MANNESMANN INTERNATIONAL GMBH, with a contract sum of USD 29,029.68. The contract was fulfilled with success in August of the same year, which represented CNOOD's one firm step of the most crucial meaning in its global business.

On December 30, 2009, the Shanghai Office of CNOOD ASIA LIMITED was established. Since then, CNOOD, with its base in Hong Kong, has had its business center in Shanghai and settlement center in Ningbo, turning a new page in the rapid growth of the company.

2010

Thanks to Dennis' one year of hard work, CNOOD's business was put on the right track after the company had been well staffed. In 2010, CNOOD became a supplier to CUNADO, MAYA ENTERPRISES, CORRTECH TRENCHLESS, and HAFFARI in succession, with the sales reaching USD700 million. In the same year, Salzgitter returned 347 million tons of goods delivered under the contract CN2010007010 (i.e. Po.504/8524) and lodged a claim for compensation.

2011

In 2011, CUNADO became our major client. In the same year, we became a supplier to ARCELORMITTAL and made new breakthrough in our business.

In 2011, CNOOD issued 10 million shares at HK$1 per share. The Shanghai Office moved from B705 to B1001 with a larger space.

2012 年

2012 年 1 月起，张召环辞去前业，结束了施璐德成立以来的兼职状态，全身心地从事施璐德财务工作。着手整理与完善施璐德公司系列操作手册，公司的财务制度体系开始系统化。

2012 年 3 月，上海施璐德国际贸易有限公司在上海成立，开始了在中国内地自营进出口业务的新局面。

2012 年下半年，公司与 GSL 成功合作，成功进入委内瑞拉市场，此后两年内，公司与 GSL 签订并完成石油套管的合同量约达 20 万吨，实现公司发展史上的第一个奇迹。

同年，CN12HE018 瓦楞板业务遭客户质量索赔 30 000 美元；CN12HA028 遭客户质量索赔 60 000 美元。

2013 年

2013 年 9 月，控股子公司 CNOOD LATAM S.P.A 在智利圣地亚哥成立，股权结构：CNOOD ASIA LTD 占 60%、MARIO HABERLET 占 10%、NICOLAS KIPREOSA 占 10%、GINO GABRIELLIM 占 10%、CRISTIAN

2012

From January 2012, Zhang Zhaohuan resigned from his previous job and thus ended his part-time work pattern since the creation of CNOOD, which enabled him to be wholly devoted to the financial affairs of CNOOD. He started systematizing and improving CNOOD's work manuals, making the financial system of the company more systematical.

In March 2012, CNOOD International Trading Company Ltd was set up in Shanghai, creating a new platform for CNOOD to carry out its own import and export business in Chinese mainland.

In the second half of 2012, CNOOD completed a successful cooperation with GSL and entered the Venezuelan Market. In the following two years, CNOOD signed petroleum casing pipe contracts with GSL and fulfilled the contract volume of approximately 200 thousand tons with the sum totaling USD 150 million, which was considered as the first miracle in the history of CNOOD.

In the same year, a quality claim of USD 30,000 was lodged by the client in the corrugated sheet business under CN12HE018. Another quality claim was lodged by the client under CN12HA028.

2013

In September 2013, CNOOD LATAM S.P.A, a holding subsidiary of CNOOD, was incorporated in Santiago, Chile, with the following shareholding structure: CNOOD ASIA LTD 60%, MARIO HABERLET 10%, NICOLAS KIPREOSA 10%, GINO

SCHOLLR 占 10%；

2013 年 12 月，公司又以每股 1 港元的价格发行股份 1 000 万股。至此，公司共发行股份 2 000 万股，实收股本金 200 万港元。

2014 年

2014 年 6 月，CNOOD HONGKONG LTD. 成立。由于质量控制问题，海运安排方面工作失误或沟通、准备不足，沙特与巴拿马市场相继出现客户索赔的情况，索赔金额达 380 000 美元。

全面整理、完善公司各项制度，转化为公司的操作手册，业务部门针对业务要点和流程，建立业务合同操作手册。

2015 年

CNOOD HOLDING LTD 成立（2015 年 4 月）；

上海施璐德海洋工程有限公司成立（2015 年 11 月 9 日）；

西班牙公司成立（2015 年 11 月）；

常熟施璐德制造有限公司雏形初显。

2016 年

2016 年 6 月，常熟公司正式建立，成为施璐德由 EPC 公司（贸易公司）向实体制造业挺进的转折性标志。

GABRIELLIM 10%, and CRISTIAN SCHOLLR 10%.

In December 2013, CNOOD issued another 10 million shares at HKD1 per share. CNOOD had thus issued 20 million shares in total with a paid-up share capital of HKD 2,000,000.00.

2014

In June 2014, CNOOD HONGKONG LTD was incorporated. In the same year, clients in KSA and Panama lodged claims for compensation totaling US$ 380,000.00, as a result of our mistakes and inadequacy of communication and preparation in quality control and shipping arrangement.

We systematized and improved all the rules and regulations of the company, and translated them into the work manual. Business departments established their business contract operation manual according to key points and processes of the business.

2015

CNOOD HOLDING LTD was set up in April 2015.

CNOOD MARITIME ENGINEERING COMPANY LTD was set up on November 9, 2015.

CNOOD ENGINEERING S.L. was set up in November 2015.

CNOOD EQUIPMENT MANUFACTURING (CHANGSHU) CO., LTD was in its embryonic form.

2016

In June 2016, CNOOD EQUIPMENT MANUFACTURING (CHANGSHU) CO., LTD was formally established, which marked a turning point in CNOOD's brave attempt

这是喜忧参半的一年。受世界经济持续低迷的影响,这一年,公司经营业绩未能止住持续下滑的势头,而各项费用却显上升态势,CNOOD 出现从 2009 年以来的首次出现亏损。

2016 年也是 CNOOD 的变革之年。CNOOD HOLDING LTD 进行了股份制改革。原持股人池勇海出售转让了其所持有的 48% 的股份,CNOOD 开启了全员持股的新时代。

2016 年,也是 CNOOD 企业管理重启顶层设计的一年,通过了《CEO 选举制度》,开始全民选举,全员治理公司的新时代。

2016 年,公司业绩虽然出现了亏损,但人员方面却出现可喜的局面,不少合伙人正式加入公司;CNOOD HONGKONG LTD 本土职员已增加 4 人,随着 Pat 的加入,CNOOD HONGKONG LTD 有了香港本土职员。

二、公司规模

2008 年

公司规模:合伙人 3 人,其他人员 1 人。

2009 年

公司规模:合伙人 4 人,其他人员 1 人。

to enter the manufacturing industry as an EPC company.

This was a year of mixed feelings for us. Influenced by the stagnant global economy during a long time, CNOOD failed to stop the decline in its business performance, while its costs and expenses were on the rise. As a result, CNOOD met with its first deficit ever since the year 2009.

2016 was also a year of change for CNOOD. CNOOD HOLDING LTD carried out a shareholding system reform, in which the original shareholder Dennis Chi sold the 48% shares previously held by him. CNOOD thus entered into a new era of employee stock ownership.

In 2016, CNOOD restarted top-level design in corporate management. "Regulation Concerning the Election of CEO" was passed, creating a new age of election and governance by all members.

In 2016, despite the deficit in the company's business performance, it was encouraging as far as the personnel was concerned. Several partners formally joined CNOOD. There were four more local employees in CNOOD HONGKONG LTD, while CNOOD HONGKONG LTD began to have local employee from Hong Kong with Pat joining it.

2. The Size of the Company

2008

In 2008, we had three partners, and one other employee.

2009

The size of the company: four partners and one other employee.

2010 年

公司规模：合伙人 6 人，其他业务助理 5 人。新入职应届毕业生 4 人，公司人才培养计划开始形成。

2011 年

公司规模：合伙人 10 人，其他业务助理 7 人，单证部成立。

2012 年

公司规模：合伙人 9 人，其他业务助理 9 人。

2013 年

公司规模：合伙人 12 人，其他业务助理 18 人。本年度，公司新入职员工中研究生以上学历的占了 70%，在学历层次上了一个新台阶，开始了公司高学历时代，为公司的发展储备提供了充足的知识资产。

年初，宁波结算中心从已度过整整 4 年的费凤家迁出，迁进靠近宁波东站的办公室，开始了真正有自己的办公室场所的时代；同时，两名新财务人员入职。

2014 年

公司规模：合伙人 19 人，其他业务助理 16 人，实习生 12 人。

2015 年

公司规模：合伙人 22 人，其他业务助

2010

The size of the company: six partners and five other business assistants. Four employees newly graduating from college joined CNOOD. The company's talent development program began to take shape.

2011

The size of the company: ten partners and seven other business assistants. The Documents Department was established.

2012

The size of the company: nine partners and nine other business assistants.

2013

The size of the company in 2013: twelve partners and eighteen other business assistants. Seventy percent of new employees who joined CNOOD this year had academic credentials above postgraduate degrees. This enabled the company to leap onto a higher level of overall educational background and enter an age of well-educated employees, preparing a sufficient equipment of knowledge capital for CNOOD's future development.

In the beginning of the year, Ningbo Settlement Center was moved into the new office near Ningbo East Railway Station from Feifeng's home, where we had worked for four years. From then on, we began to have our own office. At the same time, two financial staff members joined the company.

2014

The size of the company: nineteen partners, sixteen other business assistants, and twelve trainees.

2015

The size of the company in 2015: twenty-

理 38 人，另外实习生 1 人。

2016 年
公司规模：合伙人 24 人，其他业务助理 44 人，实习生 9 人。

三、财务部发展历程

2013 年 2 月，在宁波火车东站旁租了一间 20 平方米的办公室，虽然逼仄阴暗，也是正式有了真正的办公地点。

招聘时所碰到之事令人感慨，前来应聘的佩佩立于门前踌躇不进；安排去上海出差的思思因担忧被拐卖而携表哥陪同。

最终 3 月初，董思思入职，任财务会计。

3 月末，姚佩佩入职，任结算人员兼财务会计。

2013 年年销售额达 90 058 965 美元，公司渐渐在发展壮大。

2014 年 2 月搬迁至市政府北部即当前办公室，宁波结算中心办公条件得到了极大的改善。

3 月王月平入职，任出纳岗位。

2015 年 11 月乐萍萍实习入职接手国内公司账务。

two partners, thirty-eight other business assistants, and one trainee.

2016
The size of the company in 2016: twenty-four partners, forty-four other business assistants, and nine trainees.

3. The History of Accounting Department

In February 2013, we rented an office of 20 square meters near the Ningbo East Railway Station. Though it was a cramped and dark room, we began to have our own office.

Here are some of the interesting things that we experienced during the recruitment: Peipei, who came for the job interview, stood at the door and hesitated to enter the room; Sisi asked her cousin to accompany her during a business trip to Shanghai because she was fearful of being abducted.

Finally, in the beginning of March, Dong Sisi joined the company as a financial accountant.

At the end of March, Yao Peipei joined the company as a settlement clerk and accountant.

In 2013, the annual sales income totaled USD 90,058,965. The company was growing steadily.

In February 2014, we moved into the office to the north of the City Hall, where we are working now. Since then, the office conditions of Ningbo Settlement Center have been greatly improved.

In March, Wang Yueping joined the company as a cashier.

In November 2015, Le Pingping joined the company as a trained and took over the

至此，财务人员岗位设置基本完整，各岗位人员基本到位，岗位职责基本明确。

随着智利、西班牙、中国内地和中国香港的公司成立，宁波财务结算中心的业务范围不断扩大，工作专业度不断提升，每位同事都在成长。

accounting business of the domestic company.

Thus the company is financially well structured and well staffed, with clear job responsibilities.

With the establishment of branches and offices in Chile, Spain, Hong Kong SAR and Chinese mainland, the scope of business for Ningbo Settlement Center has been expanding all the time. With the growth of every colleague, we are becoming more and more professional.

图书在版编目(CIP)数据

施璐德年鉴.2016/施璐德亚洲有限公司编.—上海：复旦大学出版社,2017.9
ISBN 978-7-309-13278-6

Ⅰ.施… Ⅱ.施… Ⅲ.建筑企业-上海-2016-年鉴 Ⅳ.F426.9-54

中国版本图书馆CIP数据核字(2017)第236022号

施璐德年鉴.2016
施璐德亚洲有限公司 编
责任编辑/谢同君

复旦大学出版社有限公司出版发行
上海市国权路579号 邮编：200433
网址：fupnet@fudanpress.com   http://www.fudanpress.com
门市零售：86-21-65642857   团体订购：86-21-65118853
外埠邮购：86-21-65109143   出版部电话：86-21-65642845
上海丽佳制版印刷有限公司

开本 787×1092 1/16 印张 13.75 字数 263千
2017年9月第1版第1次印刷

ISBN 978-7-309-13278-6/F·2407
定价：68.00元

如有印装质量问题，请向复旦大学出版社有限公司出版部调换。
版权所有 侵权必究